Social Studies and Me!

Using Children's Books to Learn About Our World

By Sally Anderson with the
Vermont Center for the Book

Welcome...

ACKNOWLEDGMENTS

I'm Growing! by Aliki is published by HarperTrophy.

Cleversticks by Bernard Ashley, illustrated by Derek Brazell, is published by Random House.

Sometimes I'm Bombaloo by Rachel Vail, illustrated by Yumi Heo, is published by Scholastic.

Mama Zooms by Jane Cowen-Fletcher is published by Scholastic.

I Love Saturdays y domingos by Alma Flor Ada, illustrated by Elivia Savadier, is published by Aladdin.

How Many Stars in the Sky? by Lenny Hort is published by Mulberry Books.

Down the Road by Alice Schertle, illustrated by E.B. Lewis, is published by Houghton Mifflin Harcourt.

This is Our House by Michael Rosen, illustrated by Bob Graham, is published by Candlewick. Text copyright © 1996 by Michael Rosen. Illustrations copyright © 1996 by Bob Graham of Blackbird Design Pty. Reproduced with permission of the publisher, Candlewick Press, Somerville, MA.

Chester's Way by Kevin Henkes is published by HarperTrophy.

Jamaica and Brianna by Juanita Havill, illustrated by Anne Sibley O'Brien, is published by Houghton Mifflin Harcourt.

Officer Buckle and Gloria by Peggy Rathmann is published by Penguin Putnam.

Guess Who? by Margaret Miller is published by HarperCollins.

Bunny Money by Rosemary Wells is published by Puffin.

I Stink! by Kate and Jim McMullan is published by HarperCollins.

The Little Red Hen (Makes a Pizza) by Philemon Sturges is published by Puffin.

My Map Book by Sara Fanelli is published by HarperCollins.

To Be a Kid by Maya Ajmera and John D. Ivanko is used with permission of the publisher, Charlesbridge.

Where Are You Going Manyoni? by Catherine Stock is published by Morrow.

SOCIAL STUDIES AND ME!

A MOTHER GOOSE PROGRAM

SOCIAL STUDIES and Me!

Using Children's Books to Learn About Our World

Sally Anderson

with the Vermont Center for the Book

Interior Illustrations by Tracey Campbell Pearson, and iStock Photography

Gryphon House, Inc.
Silver Spring, MD

Published by Gryphon House, Inc.
10770 Columbia Pike, Silver Spring, MD 20901
301.595.9500; 301.595.0051 (fax); 800.638.0928 (toll-free)

Visit us on the web at www.gryphonhouse.com

Library of Congress Cataloging-in-Publication Data
Anderson, Sally.
 Social studies and me! : using children's books to learn about our world / by Sally Anderson and the Vermont Center for the Book.
    p. cm.
 Includes bibliographical references.
 ISBN 978-0-87659-331-8
1. Social sciences--Study and teaching (Early childhood)--Activity programs. I. Vermont Center for the Book. II. Title.
 LB1139.5.S64A53 2011
 372.83'044--dc22
                                        201004554

Bulk Purchase
Gryphon House books are available for special premiums and sales promotions as well as for fund-raising use. Special editions or book excerpts also can be created to specifications. For details, contact the Director of Marketing at Gryphon House.

Disclaimer
Gryphon House, Inc. and the author cannot be held responsible for damage, mishap, or injury incurred during the use of or because of activities in this book. Appropriate and reasonable caution and adult supervision of children involved in activities and corresponding to the age and capability of each child involved is recommended at all times. Do not leave children unattended at any time. Observe safety and caution at all times.

TABLE OF CONTENTS

CHAPTER 1

Welcome!

WELCOME TO *SOCIAL STUDIES AND ME!*

This book will support and enhance the work you are already doing with young children. It contains hundreds of ideas for using high-quality picture books, good conversations, and lively explorations that incorporate the skills, concepts, and standards of social studies, language, and literacy.

In addition, this book will help you work with children in ways that are interesting and fun to them and sensitive to their developmental needs.

Young children are naturally compelled to investigate the world around them. They are learning to understand who they are, who their family members are, and what it means to have friends. They are curious about their communities, who lives and works there, how products are made, and what things cost. They wonder about their environment and the greater world.

You can support this social studies and literacy learning by providing the tools and activities to create a learning environment that supports children's development. By observing and documenting this learning, you can share with administrators, peers, and families the learning that is taking place within each child.

Social Studies and Me! will enhance your work with young children by helping you to:

○ Identify and expand social studies themes and concepts in your interactions with children,

○ Use picture books and related explorations to promote conversations, language skills, and higher order thinking,

○ Engage children in hands-on activities that help them understand social studies and literacy skills,

○ Learn how to use social studies and literacy standards to inform your work with children,

○ Ask open-ended questions,

○ Observe individual children and groups of children more carefully,

○ Learn ways to communicate to families the work you are doing with their children, and

○ Enjoy your time with children and continue to grow in your profession.

HOW THIS BOOK IS ORGANIZED

Social Studies and Me! will help you build on what you already know about social studies and literacy. Using this book will help you work with children with more intention, talk about your work with more clarity, and address standards more thoroughly.

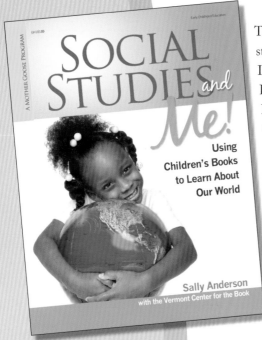

This book is organized into five sections. Each section focuses on a social studies theme:

I Am a Person
Families
Friends
Communities
The Big World

Each section begins with a general introduction to the theme:

How does this theme spark children's curiosity and interest?
How does the theme encourage children's development?
How does the theme integrate literacy and social studies?
How do the books relate to the theme?

The introduction to the theme is followed by a Book Talk and two engaging Explorations.

BOOK TALK

Each time a new book is introduced, a synopsis of the book links the story to the theme. Additional support for sharing the book with children and building literacy skills includes:

Vocabulary
O Introducing new words and concepts from the story

Objectives
O Matching the literacy standards you need to teach

Making Connections
O Suggestions for linking the book to children's experiences
O Strategies for introducing the book to children

Introducing the Book
O Tips for the initial reading of the book
O Ideas for subsequent readings of the book

Reading and Talking Together
O Ways to foster standards-based discussion and conversation about the book
O How to observe and assess learning
O Ideas for extending the learning
O Suggestions for connecting with families

EXPLORATIONS

Explorations are experiences that actively engage children in social studies and literacy learning. They are child-centered, build children's self-confidence, and deepen understanding of skills and concepts.

Explorations are divided into four steps:

1. What's Needed
O Materials needed to do the exploration
O What you'll want to think about before beginning the exploration
O Key objectives

2. Step by Step
O Clear, step-by-step instructions and helpful hints
O Tips for talking with children, including open-ended questions and comments to stimulate children's language and thinking during the exploration
O Questions to ask yourself about children's language and behaviors as you observe and assess their learning

3. Extend Children's Learning

O Ways to deepen and enrich children's social studies learning

4. Connect With Families

O Ideas for displaying children's work

WHY USE PICTURE BOOKS TO EXPLORE SOCIAL STUDIES?

Stories are a powerful way to introduce social studies to children. Stories bring social studies to life. They can help children learn how to use social studies skills and knowledge to address their own real-life problems. At the same time, children are developing critical language skills. Picture books:

O Provide a story context for social studies content,

O Encourage children to recreate stories in their own way, as well as to practice social studies skills,

O Pose problems that can be explored using a variety of real-world strategies,

O Encourage the use of social studies language,

O Allow you to modify story situations to develop social studies thinking,

O Introduce vocabulary related to social studies themes,

O Help children understand themselves and others,

O Help children make sense of their world and their place in it,

O Explore different cultures, language, and traditions through stories, and

O Promote problem-solving skills.

You will find a comprehensive list of recommended picture books for each theme in the Bibliography at the end of this book. You can also search for picture books at www.mothergooseprograms.org, using keywords such as *economics*, *community*, or *social studies*.

THE NATURE OF LEARNING IN EARLY CHILDHOOD SETTINGS

For young children, learning takes place everywhere and all the time. What the children do and say helps an observant teacher understand what the children are thinking and their degree of comprehension. As you interact with the children, you can support children who struggle with the concepts or challenge others with activities that encourage higher level thinking and additional exploration.

A single activity provides opportunities for learning in a variety of skill areas. The examples that follow illustrate some real life teacher observations and the corresponding skills and concepts children are practicing.

SOCIAL STUDIES AND ME!

What You See and Hear	Skills and Concepts Children Practice
Kyla does the same drawing of her family several days in a row.	Repeating actions over and over
Anna always checks to see which shoes Madison wears to school.	Exploring similarities and differences
Jacob asks: "Where do people eat with chopsticks? Can I find the place on our map?"	Asking questions
Jenna Mei makes a zooming machine that helps her clean up the block area quickly.	Using materials and tools in creative ways
Brianna says: "Five children in this class live in apartments."	Reporting observations
Joseph guesses that the firemen live at the firehouse.	Predicting
Anna suggests that the rules for the block center are unfair.	Problem solving
Carlos draws a map of the classroom and puts a sticker on each learning center.	Substituting symbols for real things
Christopher tells some friends that even though Africa is different in many ways from the United States, children still go to school. there.	Making connections between and among different contexts
Hannah wants to read *Cleversticks* after reading *Down the Road*.	Observing similarities and differences
Ella sorts dress-up clothes according to season.	Categorizing

WHY TEACH SOCIAL STUDIES TO YOUNG CHILDREN?

The National Council for Social Studies (NCSS) defines social studies as "the integrated study of the social sciences and humanities to promote civil competence." NCSS also asserts that the main purpose of teaching social studies is "to help young people develop the ability to make informed and reasoned decisions for the public good as citizens of a culturally diverse, democratic society and an interdependent world."

Very simply, social studies is the study of people and how they live. Young children are curious about themselves, the people around them, and the world in which we all live. Consider what most young children already know about the following "people" topics.

PEOPLE HAVE INDIVIDUAL IDENTITIES.

People are similar to each other in some ways but different in other ways. People begin as babies and grow up to be adults. People have different hair, eye, and skin colors. We speak different languages and wear unique clothing. We have similar needs for food, shelter, and attention, but we have a wide range of preferences and feelings. People are always learning and changing. Each person is an individual with his or her own personality and identity.

PEOPLE LIVE IN GROUPS CALLED FAMILIES.

People who care about each other are a family. Families may be big or little, with people who are old, young or in between. Sometimes animals are part of a family, too. Families often do things together: they have fun; they work; they solve problems; they laugh; they cry; they celebrate special days; and they care about each other. No two families are exactly the same.

PEOPLE HAVE FRIENDS.

Friends play together, talk together, giggle together, and sometimes get mad at each other. Friends should respect each others' differences and respond sympathetically to each other. Having friends makes most people feel special.

PEOPLE LIVE IN COMMUNITIES.

There are many types and sizes of communities: big cities, small towns and villages, a neighborhood, a school. Some communities have roads and buildings—homes, factories, stores, restaurants, and offices. People in communities have rights and responsibilities. They work together to help one another get the things they want and the things they need. They make and obey rules, respecting each other's individual differences.

SOCIAL STUDIES AND ME!

PEOPLE LIVE ALL OVER THE PLANET EARTH.

People live in countries near and far away. Flat places and hilly places, wet places and dry places, cold places and hot places, all are homes for our neighbors. Their houses are as different as the people who live in them: wood or brick houses, mobile homes, apartments, boats, adobes, igloos, and grass huts. People live in different ways depending on where their homes are. Each has a responsibility to take care of the Earth.

Social studies is about people and how they live. By engaging our children in real-life experiences similar to those that people have every day all over the world, they learn about some impressive-sounding topics—humanities, anthropology, geography, civics, economics, and history!

Social studies is also about helping children become involved and responsible citizens. The groundwork for that goal is laid firmly when young children are exposed to educators who can do four things:

O Make social studies topics interesting and real,

O Help children articulate their own social studies questions and pursue answers,

O Talk with children in ways that require thinking about people and how they live, and

O Observe and recognize social studies learning when children demonstrate it.

Young children have an insatiable curiosity and interest in the world around them. At an early age, they have already gathered a wealth of experiential information about their world. Their knowledge and understanding can be extended and deepened by teaching them to become social studies researchers. Social studies researchers:

O Pose questions,

O Make observations,

O Organize information, and

O Offer explanations.

As young children work, play, move, create, sing, and build their brains, they:

O Gather new information and vocabulary,

O Notice similarities and differences,

O Make connections to other experiences,

O Wonder about questions,

O Think of explanations,

O Solve problems, and

O Create generalizations or conclusions.

Social Studies and Me! is designed to focus on teaching these skills and to bring social studies into the early childhood curriculum in appropriate and effective ways.

SOCIAL STUDIES STANDARDS

Increasingly, educators are accountable for incorporating social studies standards into their work with children. Standards guide instruction, providing a framework of age-appropriate goals for teaching social studies content. Standards are designed to answer these questions:

What should children learn?
When should they learn it?
What outcomes can be expected?

The National Council for Social Studies (NCSS) has identified 10 themes around which social studies instruction can be organized. Under each theme, you will find a series of standards.

INDIVIDUAL DEVELOPMENT AND IDENTITY

For young children, this includes:
• Describing characteristics of self,
• Comparing the ways they are similar to and different from others,
• Understanding the basic needs and wants of themselves and others,
• Observing and trying to understand the behavior of siblings, peers and adults,
• Remembering the past and imagining the future,
• Comparing patterns of behavior evident in age and ability,
• Exploring, identifying and analyzing how individuals relate to one another,
• Developing a personal sense of history by examining evidence of change over time (photos of self, sorting outgrown clothes, etc), and
• Placing individual and family experiences in historical time and place.

INDIVIDUALS, GROUPS, AND INSTITUTIONS

For young children, this includes:
• Exploring the interactions among and within various groups and institutions (families, schools, churches, government agencies, and the courts, for example) that affect their lives and influence their thinking, and
• Understanding family structures, careers, and roles.

PEOPLE, PLACES, AND ENVIRONMENTS

For young children, this includes:
• Using personal experiences as a basis for exploring geographical concepts and skills,
• Matching objects to geographical locations (sorting tools, people, and so on),
• Mapping (neighborhood, classroom, and so on),
• Using spatial and location words,
• Talking about and dramatizing transportation, including how animals move, and
• Exploring similarities and differences between their own environment and other locations.

CULTURE

For young children, this includes:
• Understanding themselves both as individuals and as members of various groups,
• Identifying and comparing the characteristics and behaviors of people in different climates, locations and societies: What's the same? What's different?,
• Exploring the cultures represented by the families in the classroom and community, and
• Understanding that there are different nations with different traditions and practices.

GLOBAL CONNECTIONS

For young children, this includes:
• Exploring issues and concerns common to people around the world, and
• Understanding that there are other nations with different traditions and practices.

CIVIC IDEALS AND PRACTICES

For young children, this includes:
• Helping set classroom expectations,
• Examining experiences in relation to expectations and ideals,
• Determining how to balance the needs of individuals and the group,
• Understanding the balance between rights and responsibilities,
• Understanding how an individual can make a positive difference in the community, and
• Understanding cause and effect and how they relate to personal experiences.

PRODUCTION, DISTRIBUTION, AND CONSUMPTION

For young children, this includes:
• Understanding the difference between wants and needs and making decisions based on this understanding,
• Exploring economic decisions and experiences,
• Observing, discussing, and dramatizing basic economic concepts such as buying and selling and producing and consuming,
• Understanding money and how it is used, and
• Identifying and discussing the duties of a variety of community occupations.

SCIENCE, TECHNOLOGY, AND SOCIETY

For young children, this includes:
• Understanding that people invent tools and machines to help them solve problems or do tasks more quickly or easily.

POWER, AUTHORITY, AND GOVERNANCE

For young children, this includes:
• Exploring fairness in their relationships with others,
• Understanding how individuals and groups work to resolve conflicts,
• Understanding and making classroom rules,
• Understanding that there can be different rules in different contexts, and
• Becoming effective problem solvers and decision makers.

TIME, CONTINUITY, AND CHANGE

For young children, this includes:
• Gaining experience with sequencing to establish a sense of order and time,
• Understanding the links between human decisions and consequences,
• Describing similarities and differences between families in the past and families today,
• Beginning to understand the measurement of time,
• Understanding how the world has changed and imagining how it might change in the future, and
• Observing and documenting changes that take place over time in their immediate environment.

EXPLORING SOCIAL STUDIES

In your everyday work with children, try to identify social studies concepts that are developmentally appropriate. Weave the social studies concepts into large and small group activities, learning centers, outdoor play, field trips, and family activities.

...by talking

In everyday conversations, use appropriate social studies vocabulary such as *same* and *different*; locational and positional words; *consumer* and *producer*; *rules*; *neighbor*; *family*; *past* and *future*; and *map*.

O

Discuss similarities and differences among children.

O

Talk about book characters who live in similar or different families, environments, or countries.

O

Engage children in discussions about family traditions, foods, and routines.

O

Incorporate children's names into familiar songs, rhymes, and stories.

O

Allow plenty of time to discuss the explorations children are doing.

O

Answer the questions children have about your indoor and outdoor environments.

O

Talk about the changes you notice in each other, your classroom, and your neighborhood.

O

Discuss rules, fairness, and responsibility.

O

Talk about jobs in families, the classroom, and the community.

...with books

Read, discuss, and display books that help children learn about environments, growth, workers, food production, and other social studies ideas.

O

Read, discuss, and display books that portray diversity in cultures, environments, and families including age, gender, abilities, race, and non-stereotypic roles.

O

Display books in several places, not just in the reading center.

O

Look carefully at the pictures in books, looking for similarities and differences between the characters in the book and the children in your class.

O

Read simple stories about life long ago.

...with activities

Plan activities that encourage cooperation and collaboration.

O

Ask community helpers to visit the classroom.

O

Encourage children to help with classroom management by watering plants, putting away blocks, organizing lunch boxes, recycling, and so on.

O

Explore your community by visiting different neighborhoods, businesses, and community helpers. Provide materials for play based on these visits. For example, after a visit to a restaurant create a mock restaurant in the dramatic play center.

O

Help children make family timelines or family trees.

O

Imagine together what life was like before telephones or television.

...through documentation

Make and display charts, lists, and maps.

O

Help children make drawings, models, and books about their explorations.

O

Describe and take photographs of changes that are taking place among the children, in the classroom, and in the outdoor environment.

O

List and illustrate rules for different classroom areas.

...by supporting social studies learning in the home

Keep portfolios of children's interests, skills, and abilities to share with family members.

O

Encourage families to talk about their own traditions and family history.

O

Invite families on field trips.

O

Inform families about the local history museums and other museums where children can observe and learn about their community.

LANGUAGE AND LITERACY STANDARDS

Language and literacy are an important component of any preschool or early elementary classroom, and building a child's vocabulary is a key component in facilitating language and literacy learning. Four key organizations have made significant contributions to our understanding of what constitutes the best in language and literacy education. They are: the International Reading Association, the National Council of Teachers of English, the National Research Council's Committee on the Prevention of Reading Difficulties in Young Children, and the National Association for the Education of Young Children. The standards that follow are based on research from those four organizations. They provide a solid framework for teaching language and literacy to young children.

LANGUAGE AND VOCABULARY DEVELOPMENT
Listening and Speaking

For young children, this includes:
• Understanding the meaning of language in everyday conversations,
• Taking part in meaningful conversations with adults about many topics,
• Asking and answering questions,
• Listening to and using new words, including nouns, verbs, adjectives, and adverbs,
• Engaging in real life experiences in order to have interesting things to think and talk about, and
• Singing songs, chanting rhymes, and doing fingerplays.

LITERACY DEVELOPMENT
Phonological Awareness

For young children, this includes:
• Playing with the sounds of language through songs, rhymes, and chants,
• Playing with both real and nonsensical rhyming words,
• Identifying words with the same beginning sound (Peter/peach), and
• Hearing the difference between words that sound very similar (boat/goat, witch/wish).

UNDERSTANDING STORIES

For young children, this includes:
• Listening to stories read from books, told orally, told with puppets or as drama, and recorded on tapes or CDs,
• Sharing their own stories and experiences orally and through artwork,
• Talking about the characters in stories, and
• Recalling the sequence of simple stories.

BOOK AWARENESS

For young children, this includes:
• Knowing where books are kept,
• Handling books properly,
• Holding a book right-side-up,
• Opening the cover of the book first, and
• Becoming aware of book parts and features (front and back covers, title page, title, author, illustrator).

BOOK EXPOSURE

For young children, this includes:
• Hearing a wide variety of books (fiction and non-fiction), stories, and poetry, and
• Hearing books and stories that reflect a wide range of diversity: racial, ethnic, language, socio-economic, gender, age, religious, and geographic.

COMPREHENSION

For young children, this includes:
• Understanding the meaning of language in everyday conversations and stories,
• Asking questions and making comments relevant to conversations and stories,
• Showing appropriate emotion during a story, for example by looking sad or laughing,
• Relating information and events in conversations and stories to their own life experiences,
• Following who said or did what in conversations and stories,
• Identifying a favorite part of a story and telling why,
• Retelling stories by looking at the illustrations, using a flannel board, puppets or stuffed animals, or through drama,
• Responding to questions about stories: open-ended questions as well as who, what, when, where, why, and how questions,
• Memorizing some of the words from a story and finishing repetitive phrases or sentences, and
• Predicting what might happen next in a story.

KNOWLEDGE OF PRINT

For young children, this includes:
• Understanding that print conveys different kinds of messages,
• Pointing to print from left to right and top to bottom as they pretend to read books,
• Asking adults to read or write signs, books, labels, and other forms of print, and
• Being aware that letters can be represented in different ways.

LETTER AND WORD AWARENESS

For young children, this includes:
• Differentiating letters and print from pictorial, numerical, and graphic symbols,
• Singing or chanting the alphabet,
• Recognizing and/or naming some letters of the alphabet (in their environment on their cubbies and artwork, as well as on games, puzzles, and signs),
• Recognizing their names and a few other key words in the environment, and
• Adding letter-like symbols and/or letters to their artwork, or making signs for block structures.

LITERACY AS A SOURCE OF ENJOYMENT

For young children, this includes:
• Choosing to look at books on their own,
• Having favorite books and asking for them to be read repeatedly, and
• Enjoying trips to the library.

EXPLORING LANGUAGE AND LITERACY

In your everyday work with children, identify language and literacy concepts that are developmentally appropriate for the children you serve. Weave the language and literacy concepts into every aspect of your day.

...by reading aloud

Read aloud to children at least twice a day.

Read to children in whole groups, small groups, and individually.

Encourage children to look carefully at the book itself: front and back cover, title page, and story illustrations.

Note the names of the author and illustrator.

Occasionally point out key features of print (left-to-right and top-to-bottom progression, spaces between words, punctuation).

Take time to introduce a new book to children: name the characters, talk about the setting, discuss the pictures, point out known words, make predictions about the content or what might happen.

Choose books that reflect the diversity of our world.

Read different kinds of stories: non-fiction, fantasy, funny, sad, rhyming, realistic, and so on.

Get to know each book before sharing it with the children.

Sit so that all children are comfortable and can easily see the illustrations.

Be dramatic! Use different voices, add sound effects, make funny or scary sounds, shout, whisper, pause dramatically or speed up when there is a lot of action, and slow down at the end of a book.

Read the same book in different ways:
• Read straight through with as few interruptions as possible,
• "Read" the pictures instead of the words,
• Before reading a page, ask children to predict what might happen, and
• Encourage children to say repeating phrases.

Re-read the same book many times.

...by talking

Help children make connections between stories and their own experiences.

Build vocabulary by discussing one or two words that might be new to the children, and use the new words as often as possible.

Engage in conversations about:
• The story's setting—where it takes place;
• The characters—what they do or say and what they are like;
• The sequence of events in the story—beginning, middle, end;

SOCIAL STUDIES AND ME!

• The problem and solution in the story; and
• How the story makes children feel.

O

Find opportunities to talk about similarities and differences in words and sounds.

O

Let children supply missing rhyming words when reading rhyming stories and poems.

O

Engage children in retelling the story.

O

Talk about the books you are reading.

O

Refer to books in your conversations with children.

O

Have brief discussions when you reach the end of stories.

O

Ask children to tell about their favorite stories at circle time.

O

Help extend rather than direct children's conversations about the stories.

...through activities

Engage children in activities related to the books you read.

O

Sing songs, play rhyming games, recite nursery rhymes, and chant poems that relate to the books you've read.

O

Help children act out favorite stories.

O

Encourage children to make up silly rhyming words and chants.

O

Play games that involve giving or following directions, introduce new vocabulary, or involve making sounds.

O

Provide materials that encourage language development such as puppets and flannel boards.

...by encouraging writing

Have a variety of writing materials available including pencils, markers, paper, blank books, and envelopes.

O

Expose children to the power of environmental print, including signs, labels, charts, posters, maps, and menus.

O

Involve children when you read and write notes that pertain to them.

O

Find meaningful ways for children to write, including making labels, signs, and writing notes to family members.

O

Make sure children see you reading and writing.

O

Notice and comment on letters and their sounds.

O

Help children write their own books.

...with displays

Display books on shelves that children can reach.

O

Display classroom books in more than one place,
rather than all of them in the book center.

O

Display letters, words, and other written symbols at children's eye level.

O

Display children's drawings and writing.

O

Write down and display children's own language.

O

Include meaningful print, such as signs and messages, in your learning environment.

...by supporting language and literacy in the home

Make families aware of their children's interests, skills, and abilities.

O

Encourage children to bring favorite books from home to share with the group,
always being sensitive to the possibility that you may have children in your group
who do not have any books at home.

O

Let children borrow favorite books to take home.

O

Let families know the hours that the public library is open and encourage them to
visit it.

O

Notify families of special programs at the library or area book stores that are
appropriate for young children.

O

Invite family members to be guest readers.

O

Tell family members about books their child really enjoys.

O

Schedule book-making workshops for families.

O

Encourage families to provide children with easy access to paper, pencils, markers,
and crayons.

OBSERVATIONS

Observation can be defined as watching and listening in order to learn about individual children. An important ingredient in the learning process is the personal connection between teachers and young children. Learning about children through careful observation is the best way to build these important personal connections.

Observations personalize the relationship between teacher and child in the following way. When you as a teacher watch children before taking action, and listen to children before asking questions or making comments, you communicate a very powerful and personal message. You are telling children: I care about you and I am interested in what you do and say.

Read the examples that follow. How do you think the teachers' observation skills influenced the children's responses? Notice that the teacher carefully uses the term "disagreement" rather than "fight" in the second example as she talks with the children. It is important to use accurate terms so that the children become familiar with them.

Tyreesha is building a multi-level building with blocks. She sits back momentarily and seems to be finished building. Her teacher has been watching and now kneels down beside her and says, "Tell me about this building, Tyreesha." The girl responds, "Lots of people live in there." As soon as the words are out of her mouth, she moves to a nearby shelf, picks up a basket, and begins placing small dolls throughout the structure.

Roberto and Ian are talking about their families. Roberto tells Ian, "I have just a mother." Ian says, "No, you gotta have a daddy. Everyone has a daddy." The teacher, Ms. Redd, listens to the two boys go back and forth, and the argument becomes a bit more heated. Ms. Redd then takes two books from a shelf and gives them to the two boys, saying, "Here are some books that will help you with your disagreement. Do you want to look at them together or would you like me to join you?"

There are situations that require stepping back from children to watch and listen without interacting with them. For example, you may want to know what activities different children are engaged in at a given moment. You might look around your room, noting that a few children are gluing stars and stripes on construction paper, two children are looking at books about zoo keepers, two children are working on an airport puzzle, and another group is building a city with blocks.

This general scan gives you important information about how children are working together in groups. However, it is up to you to be aware of what is happening with each individual child.

Consider the individual variations among the children building with blocks in the following examples. What can you learn about each child's understanding of math and science?

> *Sarah uses four long blocks to make a square on the floor.*
> *She fills it in with smaller blocks in a brick-like pattern.*
> *She tells her friends, "I'm making a big parking lot for all the people's cars."*

> *Tyler connects a combination of straight and curved blocks end-to-end.*
> *He places small cars and trucks on this "road."*

> *Peter works on a tall structure. He stacks blocks that are about 10" long*
> *in a crisscross pattern and counts the layers.*
> *He says the building will touch the moon when he's done.*

> *Rosa uses 3" x 3" square blocks and slightly larger pieces of paper*
> *to make a row of 10 enclosures. They are all the same, with four sides*
> *and a piece of paper on top. Each little structure has one or more toy people inside.*
> *She tells her friends, "This is where a million people live.*
> *Now I'm going to make a supermarket so they can get food!"*

Since one goal of observation is to establish closer bonds with children and find out about their individual learning styles, pay close attention as they work and talk. What you see and hear will influence how you help them learn. For different children you may decide to change:

O The kind of questions you ask,
O The way you answer their questions,
O The type of assistance you offer,
O The ideas you share,
O The information you give, or
O The materials you provide.

With these thoughts about observation in mind, each investigation in this book includes a section called "Observe Children," which includes some guiding questions to help you notice the social studies behaviors and language you can expect to see young children demonstrate.

SOCIAL STUDIES AND ME!

DOCUMENTATION

Careful documentation of the events, projects, assessment checklists, and other pertinent information about each child is a critical element in helping you understand where a child is on the learning continuum. These records help teachers, administrators, and parents to understand each child's strengths and weaknesses, learning styles, and interests. Documentation plays an important role in planning your approach to meeting individual needs. In this book, three kinds of documentation are discussed—public, professional and assessment documentation—each one having a slightly different purpose.

PUBLIC DOCUMENTATION

Public documentation is a way to share learning experiences and activities with others, including the children themselves, their families, and other professionals. This type of documentation often takes the form of displays of children's work, actions, and language, accompanied by a written explanation of their educational significance. Some examples of public documentation include:

O Drawings and paintings with children's transcribed explanations,
O Displays of sculptures, structures, mobiles, and models with lists of the materials used,
O Sketches of block structures or designs with children's words about the problems they solved,
O Photographs of field trips with a written account of the experience, and
O Graphs showing the results of a survey about "Favorite Food" conducted by children.

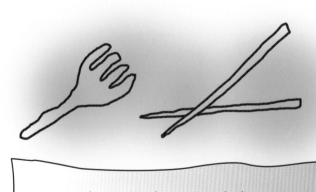

I eat with a fork. Chan eats with chopsticks.

PROFESSIONAL DOCUMENTATION

Professional documentation is intended for an educator's personal use and professional development. It includes strategies to use for reflection and planning. Two tools that help you engage in this kind of documentation follow.

O Reflective journals are records of the experiences and activities you observe in classroom learning situations, as well as your thoughts, questions, opinions, and responses to those events.

O Webs are graphic organizers that help you, the teacher, generate ideas for learning experiences that are connected to one another, making them more meaningful to young children.

ASSESSMENT DOCUMENTATION

Assessment documentation is a term used to describe the records teachers keep as they observe an individual child's actions and language. These records are used as data to help a teacher make overall decisions or judgments about a child. Conferences with family members and written reports are much more informative when specific, factual examples are used to support broad, general statements.

There are two main types of assessment documentation:

O Observational data —brief, written descriptions of a child's significant actions, language, and expressions, and

O Portfolios—collections of children's work (actual samples or photographs) that show performance and progress in key learning areas

The "Observe Children" sections of this book help you know what to focus on as you gather assessment documentation.

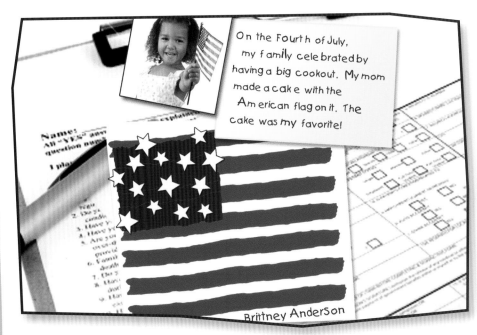

On the Fourth of July, my family celebrated by having a big cookout. My mom made a cake with the American flag on it. The cake was my favorite!

Brittney Anderson

SOCIAL STUDIES AND ME!

Graphic Representation

Charts and other graphic representations are useful tools that help young children organize, analyze, and understand information in a visual form. For the youngest children, graphic representation can be a simple drawing. Some of the Explorations in this book feature data collection and graphic representations. Data can be collected in a variety of ways and these representations help children answer questions, visualize data, and make comparisons and predictions. Some examples follow.

T- Charts help us analyze the characteristics of two objects or events and record the similarities and differences.
Bar Graphs help us compare quantities. We can visualize relationships of less than, more than, or the same as.
Block Bar Graphs are three-dimensional bar graphs using building blocks or linking cubes to represent the numbers of objects being graphed.
Pictographs are similar to bar graphs but pictures are used instead of blocks or linking cubes to represent individual objects being graphed.
Pie or Circle Graphs show how the whole collection of data is divided into parts or fractions having specific attributes.
Sorting Loops are hoops, or circles made of shoelace, yarn, or string, which are used to define sets of objects that have been sorted.
Tally Charts provide spaces for counting and recording objects. Each mark on a tally chart represents one object.
Concept Maps are diagrams that show the relationships among themes and ideas.

Many measuring devices display information in a graphic manner. Thermometers, calendars, schedules, and clocks all are visual representations of data.

Examples of graphic representation follow.

Birthday Pictograph
Jan
Feb
Mar
Apr
May
June
July
Aug
Sept
Oct
Nov
Dec

When are our birthdays?

Children participate in making a pictograph, placing a figure in the column next to the month in which they were born. When the pictograph is completed, you may wish to ask questions such as the following:

Which month has the most birthdays?
Which has the least?
How do you know?
Is there a month when no one has a birthday?
Are there months with the same number of birthdays?

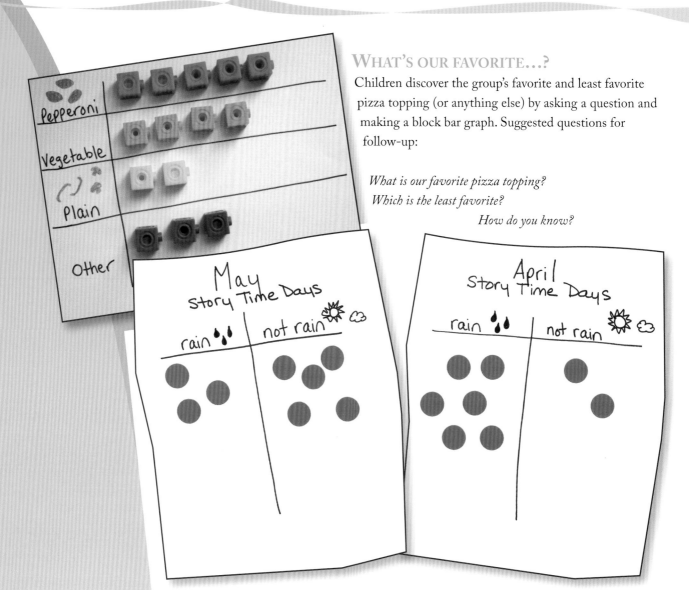

WHAT'S OUR FAVORITE…?

Children discover the group's favorite and least favorite pizza topping (or anything else) by asking a question and making a block bar graph. Suggested questions for follow-up:

What is our favorite pizza topping?
Which is the least favorite?
How do you know?

HOW MANY…?

Children collect data about the weather. They place a chip on the appropriate column of a T-Chart to compare the number of days it rained versus the number of days it did not rain. Use these questions to compare the data:

What do you notice about our T-charts?
In April, did we have more days with rain or without rain?
How do you know?
Which month had the most rainy days?

WHERE WERE WE BORN?

Children make a "live" pie graph to see where children were born.

To make the graph:
1. Everyone born in our state (the state where the school is located) stands together to form a set (group).
2. Everyone born in another state forms a set.

SOCIAL STUDIES AND ME!

3. Everyone born in another country forms a set.
4. Children in each set join hands. Then, the three sets come together to form a circle (see illustration).
5. Place a long piece of colored yarn around the outside of the circle.
6. Complete the live pie graph by placing yarn from the center of the circle to the edge of the circle, dividing the sets.

Extend the activity by asking:

What do you notice about our graph?
Where were most of you born?
How do you know?
What else can you tell from looking at our graph?

CONNECT WITH FAMILIES

Each investigation in this book includes a section called "Connect with Families." These sections will give you plenty of ideas on how to let families know about the learning experiences their children are having and offer creative ways for families to be involved.

Here are some other ways to connect with families and keep the lines of communication open:

INFORMAL CONVERSATIONS

In many schools or centers, family members drop off and pick up children. These are perfect opportunities to share interesting observations about their children. During these conversations, invite families to visit the classroom, ask questions and gather information about their child's interests, and share activities, projects, or special events that involve the child. If you do not see a parent or guardian regularly, you might want to telephone them to share positive news.

FAMILY CONFERENCES

Scheduling formal conferences enriches communication with families by allowing time for detailed discussions about learning and creative problem solving. This is an opportunity to show families examples of the explorations that their children enjoy and what they've learned by doing them. Display the child's portfolio and other documentation you have assembled to demonstrate the child's progress. Focus on the positive, highlighting the milestones met.

NEWSLETTERS

One of the best ways to communicate with families is through a newsletter. Newsletters can be sent home with children or transmitted electronically to families with computers. The best newsletters have a balance between program information

from the teacher and examples of children's work. Here are some ideas for newsletters:

○ List the books you have read and the explorations you have done.
○ Add scanned or photocopied examples of children's work.
○ Put quotes from individual children in the newsletter. Be sure to include a quote from each child at some point.
○ Using the language from the "Connect with Families" sections in this book, describe activities children have done and offer a simple way for families to try them at home.
○ Include information on upcoming events such as field trips, programs, and Family Social Studies nights.
○ Recognize and thank families who contribute in any way.

BULLETIN BOARD

A family bulletin board has two important functions. One is to get information to families that you want everyone to see, such as "Field Trip Next Week! Bring Boots!" The other function is to promote what is happening in your program. You may want to list the most recent exploration your group has done, using suggestions from the "Connect with Families" sections of this book. Post children's artwork, writing samples, and photographs of the children working in the classroom.

FAMILY EXPLORATION KITS FOR THE HOME

To extend children's learning into the home, send home an exploration kit in a small bag. This could be something you prepare in advance with a book, materials, and written instructions on how to do the exploration. An exploration kit can be an extension of an activity that has already been done in your group or it can be a completely new activity using the same book.

FAMILY SOCIAL STUDIES NIGHTS

A Family Social Studies Night is a good way to introduce families to the excitement of what is happening in your program.

Consider presenting open-ended social studies explorations for families to try. Remember, some adults may not have had good experiences with social studies when they were in school, and may be hesitant to participate. This is an opportunity to introduce social studies concepts and skills to family members and to help them learn, just as the children are learning, that these skills are already part of their daily life and that they can be opportunities for fun.

Send home invitations to the Family Social Studies Night in advance, letting families know what to expect. This might also be an opportunity to ask parents to contribute any needed materials.

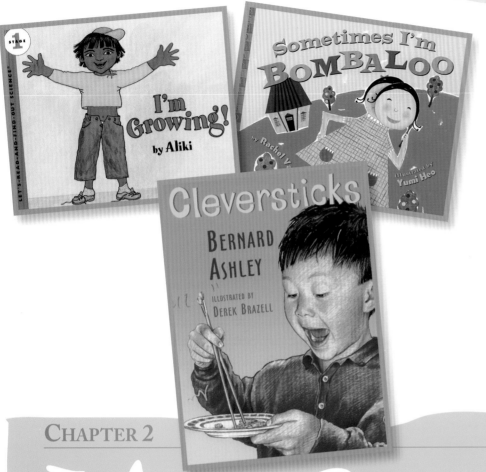

I'm Growing!
by Aliki

Cleversticks
by Bernard Ashley
Illustrated by Derek Brazell

Sometimes I'm Bombaloo
by Rachel Vail
Illustrated by Yumi Heo

CHAPTER 2

I Am a Person

INTRODUCING THE THEME

SPARKING CURIOSITY

A child's starting place for the journey into this very big world is an understanding of self. First, children learn about their own bodies, feelings, actions, and growth. Then they begin to notice those same things in other people. Gradually, they become tuned in to both the obvious and the subtle ways people are the same and different.

"Point to your eyes. Point to Mommy's eyes. Point to your nose. Now point to Daddy's nose. Point to your ears. Point to your dolly's ears!" Perhaps few families realize that when they play this time-honored game with their toddlers, they are actually beginning to teach social studies!

Consider these images of three-, four-, and five-year-old children:

o Ashley, sporting a new haircut, greets her friend Dylan at the door, exclaiming, "Now we have the same kind of hair!"

o Joseph watches in silence as a deaf classroom visitor uses sign language. The next day, his teacher notices that he makes simple gestures as he speaks.

o Mei-Mei draws two people, carefully adding arms, legs, facial features, and clothes to both, but making them different in size, color, and gender.

o Luis holds Granny Dot's hand and looks closely at her wrinkled skin before asking, "Did you stay in the bathtub too long?"

o Makaila raises her hand to share at circle time. "I can sing the same song in two kinds of words. Wanna hear?" She proceeds to sing "Frère Jacques" in both French and English.

o Madison tells everyone: "Now I can zip my own jacket!"

o At lunch time, James regularly chooses to sit beside his Japanese classmate, Koki. One day Koki asks James, "Why do you always sit with me?" James responds, "You bring pretty food."

BUILDING BACKGROUND

Every day, and probably many times during each day, the children you teach reveal their budding awareness of human appearance, feelings, habits, and behaviors. This shows how they are building their knowledge of people and the world. For example:

o They might pose a question about a person's disability,

o They might observe another child's unique approach to putting on a jacket,

o They might record their observations by drawing a picture or sculpting with clay,

o They might organize information by putting all of the girl puppets on one shelf and the boy puppets on another,

o They might offer explanations by telling why a friend was crying on the playground, and

o They might explain why they are angry about a classmate's destruction of a project.

Some ideas to start you thinking about social studies:

Idea As children engage in the explorations that are included in this section, keep asking yourself two questions related to their social studies learning:

o *What social studies knowledge do the children have?*

o *What social studies process skills are they using?*

Idea Attach a photograph of each child to an index card with his or her name on it. Use the cards to create a bulletin board display. Refer to the bulletin board frequently to begin discussions about the children, which might include their names and identifying characteristics. Rearrange the photographs to group children according to specific attributes, or frame a specific photo each day and celebrate what's special about that child.

Some ideas to start you thinking about language and literacy:

Idea

One of the most powerful strategies teachers can use to help young children recognize the power of language and print is to write down the words children say. This is called transcribing. Listen for children's interesting comments and questions as they talk about books and activities, and try to record one or two each day. It makes a child feel proud when you say, "Wait just a second. I want to write down what you just said. That was very interesting!"

Idea

Does using rhymes and poetry in the early childhood setting sound like a tall order? It may be a change for you, but it has some great benefits. Poetry helps introduce children to new ideas and concepts, and helps them express what they are feeling. Research reveals that hearing and reciting Mother Goose rhymes can help young children become successful readers.

Poem:

Yes, I Can!

I can tie my shoelaces,
I can brush my hair,
I can wash my face and hands
And dry myself with care.

I can brush my teeth, too,
And fasten up my frocks,
I can dress all by myself
And pull up both my socks.
　　　　　—Traditional

BOOK TALK

The food we eat helps our bones and muscles, skin and hair, teeth and toenails grow bigger and longer and stronger. Inside and outside, we grow and grow without knowing it! In this book, a young boy shows us how he's growing and changing while the author explains why.

Vocabulary

change: to make different in some way

grow: to expand or become larger in any way

Social Studies Standard

Individual Development and Identity

○ Describing characteristics of self

○ Comparing patterns of behavior evident in age and ability

MAKING CONNECTIONS

Before you read the book, talk with the children about their bodies and how they have grown. Display a baby doll. Explain that we were all babies once. Ask the children to share what they were like as babies including what they looked like, what they ate, and what they could do. Then ask:
In what ways do you look different now than you did when you were a baby?
How can you tell that you are growing?
What can you do now that you couldn't do as a baby?
What are some of the things that you do the same now as you did then?

INTRODUCING THE BOOK

Together, look at the cover of the book *I'm Growing!*. Tell the children that the pictures on the cover provide hints that tell us what the book is about. What do the children notice about the little boy and what he's wearing? Point to the words in the title as you read them aloud. Ask: *How can you tell this boy is growing?*

Talk about the title page of the book. The boy is holding a photograph of himself. Ask: *How is the boy different in the photograph?*

READING AND TALKING TOGETHER

○ This is a non-fiction book. Non-fiction books present facts and drawings or photographs about a subject. You can pick and choose sections of this non-fiction book to read aloud with the children. Non-fiction books aren't necessarily meant to be read out loud from cover to cover.

○ As you read, pause to give the children time to look closely at the illustrations and talk about what is happening on each page. Encourage them to use the words grow and change.

○ Can the children tell you about any other changes in their own lives as they grow: changes that are not covered in the book? Examples might be: getting eyeglasses, learning to eat with chopsticks or a fork, losing a tooth, learning to play soccer, or learning to tie a shoe.

○ Look at the author's biography in the back of the book. Share some of the information with the children. If they wrote a book, what would they like to say about themselves? Record their answers on chart paper.

SOCIAL STUDIES AND ME!

EXPLORATION:
"I'M GROWING!" BOOK

Encourage children to work together to make an *I'm Growing!* book that shows how they are different now from when they were babies.

THINGS TO CONSIDER

Begin this exploration with a general discussion about when the children were very young. For example, you can begin by saying: *When I was a baby, I had really tiny feet. Look at my feet now.*

STEP BY STEP

1. Ask the children:

   What do you know about when you were a baby?
   Are there special things only babies are allowed to do?
   What can you do now that you could not do when you were a baby?
   What is special about being big?
   Are some of the activities you did when you were a baby the same as the ones you do now?
   How do you think you'll be different when you're an adult?

2. Ask the children to help you fill in a "When I Was a Baby, Now I'm Growing" chart.

Child	When I was a baby	Now I'm growing!
José	Slept all day	Play all day
Emily	Used diapers	Use toilet
Maria	Rode in a stroller	Ride a bike

3. Invite each child to draw or cut and paste pictures to make a page for the class book. On the front of the page, they should show what they did as a baby. On the back of the page, children should show what they do now that they're bigger. Children can give you the words to write for the captions or copy them from the chart.
4. Put the pages together into a big book. If you use a binding that is easy to take apart, such as punched holes with rings or laces, you can add a second page for each child later in the year (Now that Maria is growing she...).

Alternatively, you could make a second book, making sure to write the date on the cover of each book.

What's Needed

the book, *I'm Growing!*
markers or crayons
magazines with pictures of
   children and babies
glue
scissors
large sheets of paper

Social Studies Standards

Individual Development and Identity

- Describing characteristics of self
- Comparing patterns of behavior evident in age and ability
- Remembering the past and imagining the future

Time, Continuity, and Change

- Developing a personal sense of history by examining evidence of change over time
- Gaining experience with sequencing to establish a sense of order and time

Talk with Children

Children may struggle as they try to capture the details of what things look like now and what they looked like in the past. Encourage the children by asking questions about their drawings. Ask: *What can you tell me about your drawing?*

If the children need help thinking about characteristics that make them big, you can help them identify those things. Ask:
What big-kid things do you do? Do you walk? Babies can't do that!
What about playing with trucks? Babies can't do that either!

Preschool children are just beginning to see themselves as "big kids." Talk with them about the ways you see them growing and help them focus on their special new skills.

Observe Children

Observe children as they work.
O Do they draw themselves differently as babies and as children?
O What features distinguish a baby in their drawings?
O What features distinguish them as big kids?
O Which children prefer to use pictures from magazines or catalogs?
O Do the children share ideas and opinions with the group?

EXTEND THE LEARNING

Share the completed big book with the class. Help each child read his page and tell about the artwork.

Engage the children in a conversation about being a grown-up. Talk about what grown-ups can do that children can't do. Then talk about what grown-ups have to do that children don't have to do.

CONNECT WITH FAMILIES

Display the chart, the class book, and *I'm Growing!* by Aliki where families can see them. Post the following on your bulletin board:

Making an "I'm Growing!" Book
We've been talking about all the things babies can do and all the things bigger children can do. We tried to remember some of the things we did when we were babies and then we told what we could do now that we're growing! We used this information to make an "I'm Growing!" book.

See page 178 for a reproducible copy of this note to families.

Talking about growing helps us explore social studies ideas like remembering the past and comparing how we change and grow, and how each of us has different strengths and challenges, likes and dislikes.

SOCIAL STUDIES AND ME!

EXPLORATION:

MEASURE ME!

Children use a non-standard unit to measure themselves, collect data, and display it on a chart. The investigation is repeated several times during the year to show changes over time.

What's Needed
the book, *I'm Growing!*
chopsticks, wooden blocks, or
    linking cubes
Note: Use larger objects for
    younger children. You will need
    enough of each unit so that
    when laid end to end they are as
    long as a child.
masking tape
chart paper

THINGS TO CONSIDER

Choose a non-standard unit for measuring, such as chopsticks, wooden blocks, or linking cubes. Use larger objects for younger children. It is important that the same object be used for all children in your group.

This is not a competition about who is tallest. This is an activity that helps children quantify size. Used over and over throughout the year, it will give children a practical way to recognize how they are growing physically. Keep your first chart so that you can add to it each time the children measure themselves.

Social Studies Standards
Individual Development and Identity
O Describing characteristics of self
O Comparing how we are similar to and different from others
O Developing a personal sense of history by examining evidence of change over time

STEP BY STEP

1. Ask one child to lie on the floor while you place masking tape to mark the child's head and feet. Have the child stand up and see how long (tall) she is.
2. Hold up the object that will be used for measuring, such as a chopstick. Ask the children to estimate how many chopsticks will fit between the two pieces of tape on the floor. Record their predictions on chart paper.
3. Help the child place chopsticks end to end from one piece of tape to the other. Explain that you are measuring how tall the child is. Encourage the children to count the total number of chopsticks.
4. Pairs of children can then take turns measuring each other in the same way. Make an "I'm Getting Taller Chart" to record the results.

Name	Object used	How many	Date
Mikel	chopstick	7	October 2
Amy	chopstick	5	October 2
Avery	chopstick	6	October 2

Ask questions to compare the results. Who is the tallest? How many chopsticks tall is he?

5. Older children may wish to measure again with a smaller, more accurate, unit such as linking cubes. Have them estimate how many cubes tall they think they are, then measure and find out. Ask: *Why do you think the number of cubes is different from the number of chopsticks?* Encourage the children to compare the size of the measuring units for a clue.

Talk with Children

Talk about the advantages of growing a little taller in terms of what children can do now. Say: *Now that you are six chopsticks tall, Grace, you can see what is on the top shelf. You couldn't see that when you were only five and a half chopsticks tall.*

Encourage the children to use words to compare measurements: *longer than, taller than, shorter than, the same as, or equal to.*

Observe Children

Notice the processes children use while measuring.

- How do they go about estimating before actually measuring? Do they take a wild guess or do they think for a while before guessing?
- Do the children make a continuous line of non-standard units that begins and ends on the pieces of tape?
- Can the children put three or more people in a sequence from shortest to tallest?
- Do they use the words *tall*, *short*, and *measure?*
- What kinds of questions are the children asking about measuring?

EXTEND CHILDREN'S LEARNING

Later in the year, have the children measure themselves again to see if there are any changes in their heights. Talk about the changes and record them on your chart. Be sure to display your updated chart so that families can see the changes.

Have the children draw or write about the changes.

Avery
I am taller now.
I used to be 6 chopsticks tall.
Now I am 6 ¼ chopsticks tall.

CONNECT WITH FAMILIES

Display *I'm Growing!* with examples of the objects you used for measuring and your "I'm Getting Taller Chart." Add a note to let families know about the learning that's taken place.

Dear Families,

We've been using non-standard units of measure to help us see just how tall we really are. This helped us understand and describe one of our physical characteristics and to talk about ways we are the same and different.

You can keep track of your child's growth by marking his height on a door or on a piece of paper taped to a wall. Make it more fun by recording the heights of every family member!

See page 178 for a reproducible copy of this note to families.

SOCIAL STUDIES AND ME!

BOOK TALK

Ling Sung does not want to go back to school because he cannot tie his shoes, write his name, or button his jacket the way some of the other children can. Then one day Ling Sung discovers he can do something special—a "cleverstick" trick that his whole class wants to try.

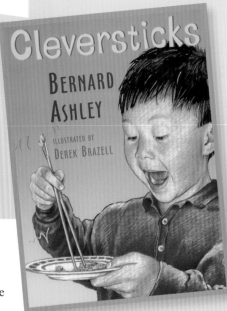

MAKING CONNECTIONS

Engage the children in a conversation about the tasks and activities they can do well. Make a chart of the children's responses, similar to the one shown here. There will be some activities many can do and some that only a few can do.

	Ana	Bobby	Derek	Yumi
tie shoes	✔			✔
hop on one foot	✔	✔	✔	✔
swim		✔	✔	✔

When you look at the chart you can ask: *What are some things most of you can do? What are some things very few of you can do? What are the things you would like to learn to do?*

INTRODUCING THE BOOK

Look at the illustration on the cover of the book *Cleversticks* together. Ask the children: *What do you think the boy is doing? How do you think the boy is feeling? What do you think might make the boy feel so happy?*

Look at the title page together. Ask: *How do you think the boy is feeling? What might make the boy feel that way? Invite volunteers to share times when they felt sad.*

Reading and Talking Together

O Read the title of the book aloud as you point to the word. Does anyone know what "cleversticks" might be? Read the book aloud to find out.

O After reading the book, compare Ling Sung's feelings at the beginning and the end of the story.
Describe Ling Sung's feelings on the first page. *What makes him feel this way?*
Describe Ling Sung's feelings on the last page. *What happens to make him feel this way?*

O Look at all the pictures that introduce tasks that a classmate can do but Ling Sung cannot do. Compare this with your class chart. Discuss the similarities and differences.

O Turn to the picture where Ling's friends are learning to eat with chopsticks. The children seem excited about learning something new. Talk with the children about other feelings they've had when they were unable to do something or were trying to do something new.

Vocabulary

chopsticks: a set of thin sticks held between the thumb and fingers used to lift food to the mouth

frustrated: feeling unsatisfied (synonyms: irritated, upset, annoyed, bothered, discouraged)

Social Studies Standards

Individual Development and Identity

O Describing characteristics of self

O Comparing how we are similar to and different from others

O Exploring, identifying, and analyzing how individuals relate to one another

Culture

O Exploring the cultures represented by the families in the classroom and community

What's Needed

the book, *Cleversticks*

cooking tools (spatula, mixing spoon, tongs, rolling pin)

cleaning tools (mop, broom, dust pan, feather duster)

drawing tools (pencil, marker, crayons, chalk)

personal hygiene tools (comb, toothbrush, floss)

building and woodworking tools (hammer, screwdriver, wrench)

Social Studies Standards

Science, Technology, and Society

O Understanding that people invent tools and machines that help them solve problems or do tasks more quickly or easily

EXPLORATION:

SORTING TOOLS

In this exploration, children explore a variety of tools, discuss their uses, and sort them by the jobs they do.

THINGS TO CONSIDER

Children will need plenty of free time to observe and handle the tools before they do a directed exploration with them.

STEP BY STEP

1. Share the picture of Ling Sung eating with his chopsticks and talk with the children about what people use chopsticks for. Then ask: *What tools do you use for eating?*

2. Display the large collection of tools. Pick up the tools one by one, inviting the children to demonstrate how the tool works and to describe what it is used for. Name each tool and agree on its use.

3. Have the children sort the tools according to their purpose, grouping tools that do the same or very similar jobs. The children may sort tools into these categories:

   drawing tools   cooking tools
   building tools   personal hygiene tools
   housekeeping tools

4. Encourage the children to think about the differences between similar tools. *When might one choose to use one or the other? What other tool could be used in its place?*

Talk with Children

As the children group the objects, engage them in meaningful conversations about the tools and encourage them to use new words related to tools. Ask:

What does this tool do?

How does a (hammer) make (building a house) easier?

Does it do anything else?

Why might people want to use this tool?

How is a saw like a screwdriver? How is it different?

Why would you choose a saw instead of screwdriver?

Observe Children

Observe and ask questions of children as they work.

O Do the children recognize the objects?

O Are they familiar with how each tool is used?

O Are they able to make connections between different tools and the appropriate jobs?

SOCIAL STUDIES AND ME!

EXTEND THE LEARNING

Make a class book of tools. Follow children's interests when deciding on the category. Some ideas: Tools for Building, Tools for Cooking, Tools for Art, and so on.

Go on a "tool hunt" in the classroom. What kind of tools do you have and what do they do?

Take one tool from your collection and talk about how it was designed to solve a problem. For example, a toothbrush was invented to help us keep our teeth clean. Brainstorm new and creative uses for a toothbrush, such as painting a wall, cleaning the floor, as a piece of jewelry, or to brush the dog. Do this with several of the tools you've explored. Be creative and silly!

CONNECT WITH FAMILIES

Display *Cleversticks* near the bulletin board with a selection of the tools used for this exploration. If you made any charts or took photographs of the children working, display those as well.

Post the following note to the parents on your bulletin board:

I Can Do It!

We've been learning about how people use tools to make their work easier. We explored real tools and sorted them by the jobs they do. We learned that:

- People create or invent tools to do specific jobs,
- Some tools can do more than one job, and
- Sometimes different tools can do similar jobs.

See page 179 for a reproducible copy of this note to families.

What's Needed

the book, *Cleversticks*

chart paper

drawing paper

markers and crayons

magazine pictures

photographs of children (optional)

Social Studies Standards

Individual Development and Identity

O Comparing how we are similar to and different from others

Culture

O Understanding ourselves both as individuals and as members of various groups

Time, Continuity, and Change

O Observing and documenting changes that take place over time in our immediate environment

EXPLORATION:

EVERYONE IS AN EXPERT

Children will make a group book detailing what each child is an expert at doing. They learn that everyone is an expert at something, and that with practice, we all become experts at new things.

THINGS TO CONSIDER

Take time to reflect on what each child in your group likes to do. Make notes of the area(s) in which each child excels and why.

Children may value different areas of expertise than those valued by adults. Kayla may be excited to share the chicken's peeping sound that she has learned to imitate, even though you value her ability to write her first and last names. Let the children write about the areas in which they feel like experts.

Do this exploration again in several months to show new areas of expertise as the children grow. This demonstrates how things change over time and shows that with practice we become proficient at new skills.

STEP BY STEP

1. Look at the pictures in *Cleversticks*. Talk about how everyone has to practice to become good at a task. Ling Sung is an expert at using chopsticks, Manjit can write her name, and Sharon buttons her coat perfectly.

2. Write "Everyone is an Expert" across the top of your chart paper. Then ask children, What are you an expert at? Write their ideas in a list.

   Susan is an expert at tying shoes.
   Luis is an expert at mixing colors.
   Jamilla is an expert at building block castles.

3. Distribute drawing paper. Encourage the children to draw pictures showing what they do well. Some children may want to cut and paste photos instead of drawing.

4. Write what the child is an expert at on his page, just as you did on the chart.

5. Put the children's pages together to make a book called "Everyone Is an Expert." Write the date on the cover. You may wish to make other books throughout the year, with the date noted on each cover so that children can compare how they've grown and changed.

Talk with Children

Draw on your knowledge of the children to help them think of what they are experts at if they are having difficulty. Describe what they do, and listen to what the children say. For example:

Stefan likes to learn Mother Goose rhymes. He is an expert at saying rhymes!

I know Marina spends a lot of time on the playground climber. She climbs to the top and then hangs by her knees, upside down. Yes, Marina is an expert at hanging by her knees.

Observe Children

Observe children as they interact with others. Take notes of specific examples to answer the following questions:

○ What do the children value expertise in?
○ How do they perceive expertise in others?
○ Do they see the things they do as practice toward being experts?
○ Do the children feel good about themselves?
○ Are they able to celebrate their classmates' successes?

EXTEND THE LEARNING

Help children make individual books called "I Am an Expert," featuring a different skill or achievement on each page.

Learn to do something new as a group. You might want to learn how to build really tall towers, bake cookies, learn a song with a fun dance or hand motions, line up for the playground quickly and quietly, do somersaults, or say "hello" in another language. Make a bulletin board display with photographs to celebrate your group's achievements.

CONNECT WITH FAMILIES

Display *Cleversticks* and the "Everyone Is an Expert" chart and class book where families can see them.

Post the following on your bulletin board:

Everyone Is an Expert

Inspired by Ling Sung in the book *Cleversticks,* we talked about all of the things we are experts at. Each child made a page in our class book to illustrate their expertise. We will add to our book later in the year to see how we have grown and changed. Things we talked about:

- Everyone is good at something,
- People have to practice a lot before they become an expert at something,
- Different people are experts at different things, and
- As people grow and change, they learn new skills and become experts at new things.

See page 179 for a reproducible copy of this note to families.

Sometimes I'm BOMBALOO

by Rachel Vail

Illustrated by Yumi Heo

SCHOLASTIC

Book Talk

Most of the time Katie Honors is a really nice girl. But when she gets very upset, she is just not herself. Sometimes, she's Bombaloo—a person who's a little out of control, using her feet and fists instead of words. Through the story and pictures we are reassured that Katie can become herself again, with a little love and some time out.

Vocabulary

fierce: showing aggression or anger

growl: to speak in a deep or rumbling voice

whine: to complain about something in an annoying voice

Social Studies Standards

Individual Development and Identity

O Describing characteristics of self

O Observing and trying to understand the behavior of siblings, peers, and adults

O Exploring, identifying, and analyzing how individuals relate to one another

MAKING CONNECTIONS

Before reading the book, have the children use their bodies to show how they look when they are angry. Talk with the children about what makes them angry, how it feels to be angry, and what they do when they are angry. Invite volunteers to share what they do or think to make angry feelings go away.

INTRODUCING THE BOOK

Before reading the book *Sometimes I'm Bombaloo*, look at the cover with the children. Ask: *What do you think this book is about? What do you think the girl on the cover is doing? What do you think she is holding in front of her face?*

Explain that the girl's name is Katie. Turn the pages of the book, and ask the children to find the word "Katie" on each page. Then read to find out why Katie is Bombaloo.

READING AND TALKING TOGETHER

Read the book straight through with few interruptions so that the children can follow the drama of Katie becoming Bombaloo and then getting back to her old self again.

Talk with the children about the name *Bombaloo*. Do any of them have a name for themselves when they feel angry? What is it?

Look at the pictures of Katie throughout the book. Ask the children: *How does she look when she is Katie and when she feels like Bombaloo? What is the same? What is different?*

Talk about the different sounds Katie makes when she is angry. Practice some of the noises with the children—growling, whining, and making other fierce noises like Katie when she is Bombaloo.

Invite the children to share sounds they make when they are happy. Practice making some of these noises.

SOCIAL STUDIES AND ME!

EXPLORATION:

SELF-PORTRAIT

Children study their own faces in the mirror and then draw a self-portrait to be displayed in a classroom portrait gallery.

What's Needed

the book, *Sometimes I'm Bombaloo*
stand-up mirrors
9" by 12" white construction paper
multicultural crayons, markers or
    paints
colored construction paper or
    picture frames

Social Studies Standards

Individual Development and Identity

O Describing characteristics of self
O Comparing how we are similar to and different from others
O Exploring, identifying and analyzing how individuals relate to one another

THINGS TO CONSIDER

This exploration requires children to stay focused for a period of time. Try to schedule it at a time of day when children are best able to concentrate. Make sure the physical space is arranged so that children are not crowded, but are able to see each other and the mirrors clearly.

If you have a large group, you may want to offer a quiet activity for some of the children during this time to avoid crowding around the mirrors.

STEP BY STEP

1. Begin this exploration with a discussion about the features of children's faces, such as eye and hair color. Continue by having them describe special items they might have on such as earrings, glasses, or hearing aids. Ask:
   What features do you see?
   What is special about the way you look?
2. Working with three children at a time (or more if you have enough mirrors), have each child sit where he can clearly see himself in a mirror.
3. Ask the children to look carefully at themselves in the mirrors: at the shape of their eyes, the color of their hair, and the color of their skin. Then ask them to draw their faces.
4. As the children complete their self-portraits, ask each of them to pick a color of construction paper for a frame.
5. Have the children hold up their pictures during group time and share one thing they like about the portrait they drew. Record their comments.
6. Set up a group portrait gallery to celebrate the unique characteristics of each child.

Talk with Children

Young artists need specific feedback regarding their work. You might say something like this:

I like the way that you looked carefully at your eye color and chose a color that matched it best.
That brown really matches your hair color!
I see you are holding something in your picture. What is it?

Encourage each child to say something positive about their friends' portraits.

Observe Children

O Some children may not be able to focus on this exploration in the way you had planned. Praise their attempts, pointing out specific things they did to stay focused.

O Watch how the children divide their time between looking at themselves and drawing. Do some create the self-portrait immediately? Do others focus on themselves in the mirror? What colors do the children use to represent themselves? Are some children more interested in what others are doing and taking cues from their work?

O The documentation you make of this exploration is important in noting each child's progress. Keep the portraits, copies of the children's comments about themselves and their portraits, and your observations in each child's social studies portfolio, along with any relevant photographs.

EXTEND THE LEARNING

Revisit this same self-portrait exploration several months or even a year later. As the children become more comfortable with drawing themselves, you might suggest they try to do a happy self-portrait, a sad self-portrait, or a portrait that tells you how they are feeling at the moment. Compare with the children how their artwork has changed. Ask them if things they like about themselves have changed.

Look back at the pictures of Katie's monster faces in *Sometimes I'm Bombaloo*. Invite the children to draw funny, monster portraits of Katie or themselves to show how their face looks when they get really angry.

CONNECT WITH FAMILIES

Display *Sometimes I'm Bombaloo* and the children's self-portraits where families can see them. Large appliance boxes make great, four-sided displays for artwork. Invite families to visit the portrait gallery.

On the wall near the portrait gallery or on one side of the appliance box, post this message:

Self-Portrait

After reading *Sometimes I'm Bombaloo*, we took time to look carefully at our faces in a mirror and drew what we saw. We talked about:

- The parts of our faces,
- How our features are the same and different,
- What we especially like about how we look, and
- What our faces can tell others about how we feel.

See page 180 for a reproducible copy of this note to families.

SOCIAL STUDIES AND ME!

EXPLORATION:

FEELINGS MASKS

Children learn to recognize feelings and represent them in masks. They talk about the feelings their masks represent, observe themselves in the mirror, and talk about how other children's masks make them feel.

What's Needed

paper plates
large paper bags
colored paper
wallpaper
yarn
chenille sticks
large wooden craft sticks
variety of art scraps
scissors
glue
markers

Social Studies Standards

Individual Development and Identity

O Describing characteristics of self
O Exploring, identifying and analyzing how individuals relate to one another

THINGS TO CONSIDER

Before you begin, talk with the children about masks. You might ask:

Has anyone ever worn a mask?

What did the mask look like?

Why are masks fun to wear?

How did you feel when you were wearing a mask?

Explain that they will be making masks today.

Having something like a paper bag put over their head may frighten some children. By offering a variety of materials, you make it possible for children to make a mask they will feel comfortable wearing.

Show a paper plate mask of a smiling girl's face. See cover of *Bombaloo* for an example. Use yarn hair, cut holes for eyes, paper scraps for other features, and a wooden craft stick to hold mask in front of face.

Show a paper bag mask of a more monster-like/grouchy face. See examples of monster faces in *Bombaloo*. Have the child wear the paper bag over his head. Use curled chenille sticks for hair, wallpaper scraps for features, other art scraps as needed to decorate.

Safety tip: Make sure masks have holes cut for eyes so that the children have a clear field of vision. An adult should assist with cutting the eye holes.

STEP BY STEP

1. Demonstrate how paper plates and large paper bags can be used to make masks. Show the children which materials have been precut for use as eyes, teeth, or hair. Point out other art materials that can be used to decorate their masks.
2. Talk about the different masks children might make: a surprised mask, a scared mask, or a happy mask.
3. Allow plenty of time for mask-making. This can be a raucous exploration, so you may need to allow more than one day.
4. After the children have made their masks, encourage them to talk with one another and ask about each other's masks.

Talk with Children

Help children make masks that express what they are feeling. Have them focus on different parts of their faces and how to use their faces to show emotions. Ask:

How does your mouth look when you are sad?
Do the sides go up or down?
Can you look surprised?
Let's look in the mirror. Tell me about your eyes.

Making masks gives children a chance to build vocabulary about their feelings. You might say:

That mask is scary. What other words can you use to describe how it makes you feel?

Observe Children

Observe children as they work. Make notes about their work habits and their progress in understanding their emotions.

O Do some children seem to know exactly what they want their masks to look like?
O Are they confident in their mask-making or do they need support in both design and method?
O When they wear their masks, do different personalities seem to jump out?
O What words do the children use to describe their emotions?

EXTEND THE LEARNING

Children may want to create a play using their masks. Encourage them to come up with a simple story that includes all the children. You could even practice it and perform it for another class or for their families.

Be sure to take photographs of the children in their masks. Display the photographs in the room, put them in the children's portfolios, or send them home for families to enjoy.

Place the art materials in the Social Studies Center and allow the children to make new masks during center time.

CONNECT WITH FAMILIES

Display *Sometimes I'm Bombaloo* and the masks where families can see them. If you have taken pictures of the children in the masks, post the photos, too. Add a note to let the families know about the learning that's taken place. The following is an example of a note to post.

Making Feelings Masks

After we read *Sometimes I'm Bombaloo* we talked about different feelings we have and how they can show on our faces. We made masks to show these different feelings. We learned to:

- ◘ Identify lots of different feelings like sad, surprised, happy, and scared,
- ◘ Make faces to show these feelings,
- ◘ Make a mask to show a feeling, and
- ◘ Act out feelings using the masks.

See page 180 for a reproducible copy of this note to families.

Mama Zooms
by Jane Cowen-Fletcher

I Love Saturdays y domingos
by Alma Flor Ada
Illustrated by Elivia Savadier

How Many Stars in the Sky?
by Lenny Hort
Paintings by James. E. Ransome

Down the Road
by Alice Schertle
Illustrated by E.B. Lewis

CHAPTER 3

Families

INTRODUCING THE THEME

SPARKING CURIOSITY

A child's education begins at home, long before he or she comes into a classroom.

A family is a child's first and most important teacher.

How many times have you heard statements similar to these? All you have to do is sit down with a young child and say, "Tell me about your family." The special place children hold in their hearts for their families will become readily apparent.

As an early childhood professional, you know that establishing connections to families is a crucial part of the learning process. Learning involves interaction among people who have emotional links with one another—acceptance, trust, appreciation, and encouragement. Since most young children already have established an emotional bond with their families, building a strong bridge

between school and home helps young children develop those same emotional links with their school. In other words, learning requires the give-and-take of a social group. The family is the first social group that most children experience. School is often next in the long line of social groups we all participate in throughout life.

Consider these typical four-year-old comments and the social studies concepts that are behind them:

○ *We don't kiss in my family. We just hug each other.*
Families are groups of people who care about each other in different ways.
○ *I have a really old person in my family; it's my great-grandmother.*
Families are made up of people of different ages.
○ *You're lucky because you have a brother and two sisters. I don't have ANY.*
Families can be quite small or very large.
○ *My Dad says that Aunt June and Uncle Hal are still my family even if they live far, far away.*
Some members of a family live together and some live apart from one another.
○ *I used to have two Grandpas, but now I only have one.*
Families change over time.
○ *We don't eat meat in my family because we're vegetarians.*
Families have different routines, habits, and celebrations.

BUILDING BACKGROUND

Young children have already absorbed a lot about their own families. They are ready to think about other families, compare and contrast families, and consider new aspects of their own families. In short, young children are ready to "study" families as part of the social studies curriculum.

Some ideas to start you thinking about social studies:

Idea Have the children make paper doll cutouts to look like themselves. Help them personalize the paper dolls by printing information on the dolls, such as their names, ages, names of family members, and pictures of where they live. Post the paper dolls around the room.

Idea Learning about families sets the stage for young children to understand many different types of social groups—schools, neighborhoods, towns, and cities. They also learn about different ways in which people interact and depend on one another.

Some ideas to start you thinking about language and literacy:

Idea
An important rule of thumb when encouraging children's language development is to let them talk about topics that are near and dear to their hearts. Family is one of those topics. Make sure to keep your study of families very personal. Thinking and talking about their own families will eventually lead children to think and talk about other children's families.

Poem:

Twinkle, Twinkle, Little Star

Twinkle, twinkle, little star,
How I wonder what you are.
Up above the world so high,
Like a diamond in the sky.
Twinkle, twinkle, little star
How I wonder what you are.

Twinkle, twinkle, little star,
How I wonder what you are.
As your bright and tiny spark,
Lights the traveler in the dark,
Though I know not what you are,
Twinkle, twinkle, little star.

—Traditional

When you begin to work with a poem, post it on your classroom wall. Share the poem with the children at group time. Notice how the children become familiar with it. Do their lips move as you read it aloud? Do their bodies move to the rhythm of the language? Track the text with your finger. Do the children point to text when they "read"? Share the poems with parents: send copies home in the newsletter, ask parents to read them with the children or even have a group recitation!

Mama Zooms
Jane Cowen-Fletcher

SCHOLASTIC

Vocabulary

disabled: a word used to describe somebody with a condition that makes it difficult to perform some or all of the basic tasks of daily life

tunnel: any passage or route through or under something

BOOK TALK

A little boy sits in his mother's lap and she uses her zooming machine to take him everywhere. Her zooming machine is really a wheelchair, but to her son it is a race car, a train, and a plane. There is no place she cannot go in her zooming machine.

MAKING CONNECTIONS

Before you read *Mama Zooms*, talk with the children about places they like to go with their families. You might ask: *Where do you like to go? How do you get there? Can you think of ways that would get you there faster? Can you think of ways that would be slower?*

Make a list of different ways to get somewhere (car, bicycle, scooter, bus, walking, train, and so on).

INTRODUCING THE BOOK

Together, look at the front cover of the book. Ask: *What do you notice about this cover? What do you think is happening here? Who do you think these people are?* Read the title aloud and ask the children to predict why Mama zooms everywhere.

Turn to the back cover. Ask: *What do you notice here? Does anyone know what this big wheel is for?*

Open to the title page and point out the collection of hats. Ask: *What are all of these hats for? Who wears each kind of hat?*

READING AND TALKING TOGETHER

○ After you have read the book aloud once, read it again. Pause to look carefully at the art and to talk about all the things Mama and her child can do together. When you get to the picture of the ramp, ask: *Why do you think they love ramps?*

○ Draw attention to each hat from the title page as it appears in the story. Talk about what hats you might wear for different occasions. Ask: *Would you wear this hat if it were raining? When you are pretending to be a cowboy? a jockey? What kinds of hats do you have?*

○ Invite children to share anything they know about people who use wheelchairs. Ask: *Do you know anyone who has a wheelchair? If someone you loved had a wheelchair, what things could you do together? Can you think of ways a person in a wheelchair would need help?*

SOCIAL STUDIES AND ME!

EXPLORATION:

HOW DO YOU ZOOM?

Children work individually or with a friend to meet a variety of "zoom challenges." A "zoom challenge" involves finding the answer to the question "How could I do X if I were limited in Y way?" The zoom challenges help children empathize with those who have difficulty accomplishing tasks many of us take for granted.

What's Needed
wheelchair
aids such as crutches, sling, cane

Social Studies Standards
Individual Development and Identity
o Understanding basic needs and wants of themselves and others
o Comparing patterns of behavior evident in age and ability

SCIENCE, TECHNOLOGY, AND SOCIETY

Understanding that people invent tools and machines that help them solve problems or do tasks more quickly or easily.

THINGS TO CONSIDER

Talking with children about the materials they might need to meet a "zoom challenge" is part of this exploration. For instance, if the challenge is trying to eat use only one arm, you may need a sling. If it is to walk with only one foot, you may need crutches.

If the children have relatives, siblings, or friends with different physical abilities this will be a very special exploration for them. Of course, if any children in the class have physical disabilities or impairments, they will be experts at different kinds of "zoom challenges" and can share their experiences.

Be sure to use "people first" language when referring to people with disabilities. For example, instead of saying Mama is handicapped or Mama is wheelchair bound, you might say Mama needs a wheelchair or Mama has a physical disability.

STEP BY STEP

1. Review with the children your discussion about *Mama Zooms* and her wheelchair.
2. Tell the children that you will be playing a game called "Zoom Challenge." The first challenge is to move across the room using only one foot. Let one child take the zoom challenge and then ask if anyone else can find another way to do the task. Tell the children that they may use any material in the classroom to help them, and that it is OK to have a friend help them out.
3. Have the children try another challenge, such as building a bridge with blocks, but using only one hand. Have the children take turns performing the task.
4. Let the children come up with their own challenges.

Talk with Children

If you have used the word disability, be sure to define it for the children. Here are two possible definitions you could adapt to your group:

O A condition that keeps a person from doing his normal activities, or one that makes it more difficult to do those activities. A disability may affect the person some of the time or all the time, or

O A physical or mental impairment that greatly limits one or more major life functions.

Ask the children questions that will help build empathy with the person taking the challenge, such as: *How would you meet that challenge? How do you think the person feels?*

Observe Children

Children may have different reactions to this activity. Some will enjoy the physical aspects of a "Zoom Challenge;" others may find it humorous to watch the problem-solving skills of their peers. Some children may feel sad about friends or family members who have difficulty with daily life activities. As the children think of possible solutions to each zoom challenge and think of other challenges, do you see them relating the challenges to those faced in *Mama Zooms*? Do you hear the children talking about actual disabilities, such as blindness or needing to walk with a cane?

EXTEND THE LEARNING

Borrow a child-sized wheelchair from the school nurse or from a neighborhood clinic or hospital. Give each child a turn moving around the classroom in the wheelchair. Ask them: *How easy is it to get around in a wheelchair? How would you get around your house if you used a wheelchair? How about around the neighborhood?*

Go for a walk with your group and look for places where it might be difficult to take a wheelchair. You could take one child in the wheelchair and experience wheelchair access as a group.

CONNECT WITH FAMILIES

Display *Mama Zooms* where families can see it. Post the following on your bulletin board:

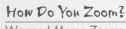
How Do You Zoom?

We read *Mama Zooms*, a book about a mother who takes her son everywhere in her zooming machine, which is really a wheelchair. To help children learn more about what life is like for people with different physical abilities, we played a game called "Zoom Challenge." In the game we tried to do things like move across the classroom using only one foot, or build with blocks using only one hand. By taking and meeting these challenges, we were able to broaden our understanding of different people's lives and develop empathy for others' experiences. We also spent time thinking and talking about how people invent tools and machines to help accomplish tasks.

See page 181 for a reproducible copy of this note to families.

EXPLORATION:

WHAT DO YOU LIKE TO

DO WITH YOUR FAMILY?

In this exploration, children will make a class book about the kinds of things they do with their families.

What's Needed

the book, *Mama Zooms*
chart paper
markers and crayons
9" x 12" drawing paper
wallpaper

Social Studies Standards

Individual Development and Identity

○ Observing the ways we are similar to and different from others

○ Remembering the past and imagining the future

THINGS TO CONSIDER

Take into consideration the developmental level of the children in your group and their comfort with drawing when you ask them to illustrate their pages in the book. Some children draw pictures that clearly represent their ideas. Other children may make drawings that look like scribbles and be thrilled with the results. Still others may say "I can't," and need a simple outline to color in or a magazine picture to cut out.

STEP BY STEP

1. Look back through *Mama Zooms* with the children, reflecting on what the little boy and his family like to do together. Recall that they like to "zoom," they like to play pretend games, they like to go for walks outside, and do other activities together.
2. Post chart paper with "What Do You Like to Do with Your Family?" written across the top. Ask the children what they like to do with their families, recording their answers on the chart paper. It may help to put your name on the chart first to model the idea for the children. "Mrs. Rathman's family likes to go hiking." Be sure to write each child's contribution with the same sentence pattern: "_____'s family likes to _____."
3. When everyone has had a chance to answer, explain that you want to make a book about what families like to do together. Children should take a piece of paper and illustrate their family's page. Write the sentence from the chart on each child's page or have them copy it.
4. Write, "We all like to do things with our families!" on the last page. Staple the pages together into a book. Be sure to add a colorful wallpaper cover so the book will be appealing and long-lasting on your classroom bookshelf.

Talk with Children

As children are sharing what their families like to do, comment on similarities and differences. For example:

Evan's family likes to go to the lake. They enjoy playing in the water like Garrett's family when they splash in the sprinkler.

Marguerite's family likes to go to the library. They enjoy a quiet activity just like Ricardo's family when they go fishing.

I notice that some families like indoor activities and some like outdoor activities.

Observe Children

Are children making connections between their family's activities and those of the other children? Watch and listen to children as they discuss the completed class book.

○ Are they noticing similarities and differences between families?

○ Do the children talk about activities they enjoy doing with their families?

EXTEND THE LEARNING

Encourage the children to think about what we do with our families and what we do at school or child care. Invite the children to act out the differences and similarities between the two environments. Provide props whenever possible. For example:

At home we eat dinner in a big chair, but at school we eat snacks in a little chair.

At home we sleep in a bed, but at school we rest on a mat.

CONNECT WITH FAMILIES

Display *Mama Zooms*, the chart, and the class book What Do You Like to Do with Your Family? Along with the books and chart, post the following information to let families know about the learning that has taken place:

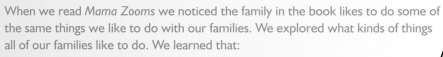

When we read *Mama Zooms* we noticed the family in the book likes to do some of the same things we like to do with our families. We explored what kinds of things all of our families like to do. We learned that:

▪ Families like to spend time together,

▪ Families enjoy lots of different things, and

▪ Families are both very similar and very different.

See page 181 for a reproducible copy of this note to families.

SOCIAL STUDIES AND ME!

BOOK TALK

The little girl in this story has two sets of grandparents. One set has a European-American heritage and speaks English, and the other set has a Mexican-American heritage and speaks Spanish. She has opportunities to visit with both, communicating in two languages and learning about ways in which her grandparents are the same and different.

MAKING CONNECTIONS

Talk with the children about their grandparents or other people in their lives older than their parents. You might ask:

Do any of these people speak a language that is different from the one you speak at home?
What language do they speak?
What are some of the words in that language?

If the children have more than one set of grandparents or other older relatives, you might ask:

What special holidays or events do they celebrate?
How do they celebrate a birthday?

INTRODUCING THE BOOK

Note: If you're unfamiliar with Spanish, practice reading the book aloud before reading it to the children.

Share the cover of the book with the children. Read the title aloud and talk about the people on the cover. Ask:

Who do you think this group of people might be?
Do some of the people look the same? How?
Do some of the people look different? How?

Explain that in this book there is more than one language, more than one name for an object, and more than one way of saying the same thing.

READING AND TALKING TOGETHER

O Read the book, having the children listen to find out about a little girl's weekends visits with different sets of grandparents.

O Talk about the activities the girl shares with each set of grandparents. Ask:
How are they different?
How are they the same?
What activities and celebrations do you share with your grandparents?

Vocabulary

language: the speech of a country, region, or group of people, including its diction, syntax and grammar

The words in English on one page are repeated in Spanish on the next page, making this a good book to begin to learn basic vocabulary in both languages. For example:
Sundays = domingos
Grandpa = Abuelito
Grandma = Abuelita
hi = hola

Social Studies Standards

Individual Development and Identity
O Exploring, identifying, and analyzing how individuals relate to one another

Individuals, Groups, and Institutions
O Exploring the interactions among and within various groups and institutions (in this case, families) that affect their lives and influence their thinking

Culture
O Exploring the cultures represented by the families in the classroom and community

FAMILIES

○ Talk about the stories the grandparents tell about where their families came from. Ask:

Do your grandparents tell stories?
What is your favorite story?
What are some of the things your grandparents do?

○ As you read, pause to compare the words in English and Spanish. Open up to a spread like the one in which the girl and her grandparents are counting. Point out how the story says: "I count them: One, two, three, four, five, six, seven, eight, nine, ten, eleven, twelve and then, I count them: Uno, dos, tres, cuatro, cinco, seis, siete, ocho, nueve, dies, once, doce."

○ Make a list of the words in English and Spanish to post in the classroom. You might add to this list as you discover other words in Spanish, or add other words that children are familiar with in other languages.

EXPLORATION:

WE TAKE CARE OF "BABIES"

Children make "sock babies" and demonstrate ways to take care of them in the dramatic play area.

What's Needed

clean socks (one for each child)
pillow stuffing
large blunt needles
yarn
non-toxic fabric paint
baby blankets, bottles, and other
   baby play accessories

Social Studies Standards

Individual Development and Identity

○ Understanding the basic needs and wants of themselves and others

○ Exploring, identifying, and analyzing how individuals relate to one another

THINGS TO CONSIDER

Be sure to use socks in a variety of colors, not all white socks, not just skin tone socks, but red, purple, gray and as many colors as you can find.

Some children may be able to "stuff and stitch" independently and others may need assistance. You may want to invite a volunteer to come in to help.

This exploration can take several days. Children may need to stuff and sew on one day and paint on another.

STEP BY STEP

1. After reading *I Love Saturdays y domingos*, ask the children about the many ways the girl's grandparents take care of her. Do a picture walk through the book to help them remember details.

2. Tell the children they will be making their own "babies" to take care of at school. Model for the children how to stuff a sock, sew it shut, and paint a face on it. Talk about what you are thinking about as you make the sock baby. For example, you might say:

   Hmm, I think it's not full enough, I'll add more stuffing.
   An eye here, another right there…I think I'll use blue for the mouth.

3. Have the children stuff their socks and sew them shut. They can then paint their dolls' faces.

4. When the paint is dry, have the children share their babies with the group. Each child can tell the group the baby's name and something about it.

5. The children should leave their dolls at school for a few days to play with them. Encourage them to use the baby accessories in the dramatic play area to take care of their babies.

Talk with Children

If there are children who are reluctant to participate in dramatic play, model baby care and talk about what you are doing. You might say:

My baby is chilly, I will wrap her in a blanket.
I hear my baby crying, I think she wants to be held and rocked.
The baby is hungry. What should we do?

Observe Children

Notice which children are comfortable in the caregiver role and which are not. Think carefully about your classroom environment; is it a place where it is all right for both boys and girls to play at being a nurturer? Do you see children being more nurturing of each other in response to this exploration?

EXTEND THE LEARNING

Write down children's My Baby Doll stories. Have them tell you about:
What my baby does,
How I take care of my baby,
What my baby likes.

Consider inviting a parent and baby to visit your class to share what mothers and fathers do to take care of their child.

Invite grandparents to join you for lunch or snacks. Encourage them to share stories about themselves.

CONNECT WITH FAMILIES

Share the children's work with their families. Make a nursery with soft blankets to display the sock babies. Set out *I Love Saturdays y domingos* and photographs of children making the baby dolls and playing with them. Post a description of the learning that has taken place. An example is below.

We Take Care of "Babies"

We've been exploring how families take care of each other. We made baby dolls and practiced caring for them. We learned:

- Adults take care of babies and children,
- Adults do things for babies and children until they are able to do things for themselves,
- People in families take care of each other, and
- It is a lot of work caring for a baby.

See page 182 for a reproducible copy of this note to families.

EXPLORATION:

WHAT'S IN A NAME?

Children discuss, collect data, and then make a pictograph to represent the different names they use for their grandparents.

THINGS TO CONSIDER

You will almost certainly have children with some grandparents who are no longer living. You could interview family members to find out the names that were used for the grandparent. Or, you might ask the child to make up names of endearment they could call a grandparent, step-grandparent, or other older adult.

STEP BY STEP

1. Review what the grandparents in this book were called (Grandma, Grandpa, Abuelita, Abuelito). Tell the children you will make a pictograph to show what names they call their grandparents.
2. Write "What do you call your grandfather?" at the top of the chart. Go around the circle, inviting each child to offer the names she calls her grandfathers. Write all the grandfather names down the left-hand side of the chart.

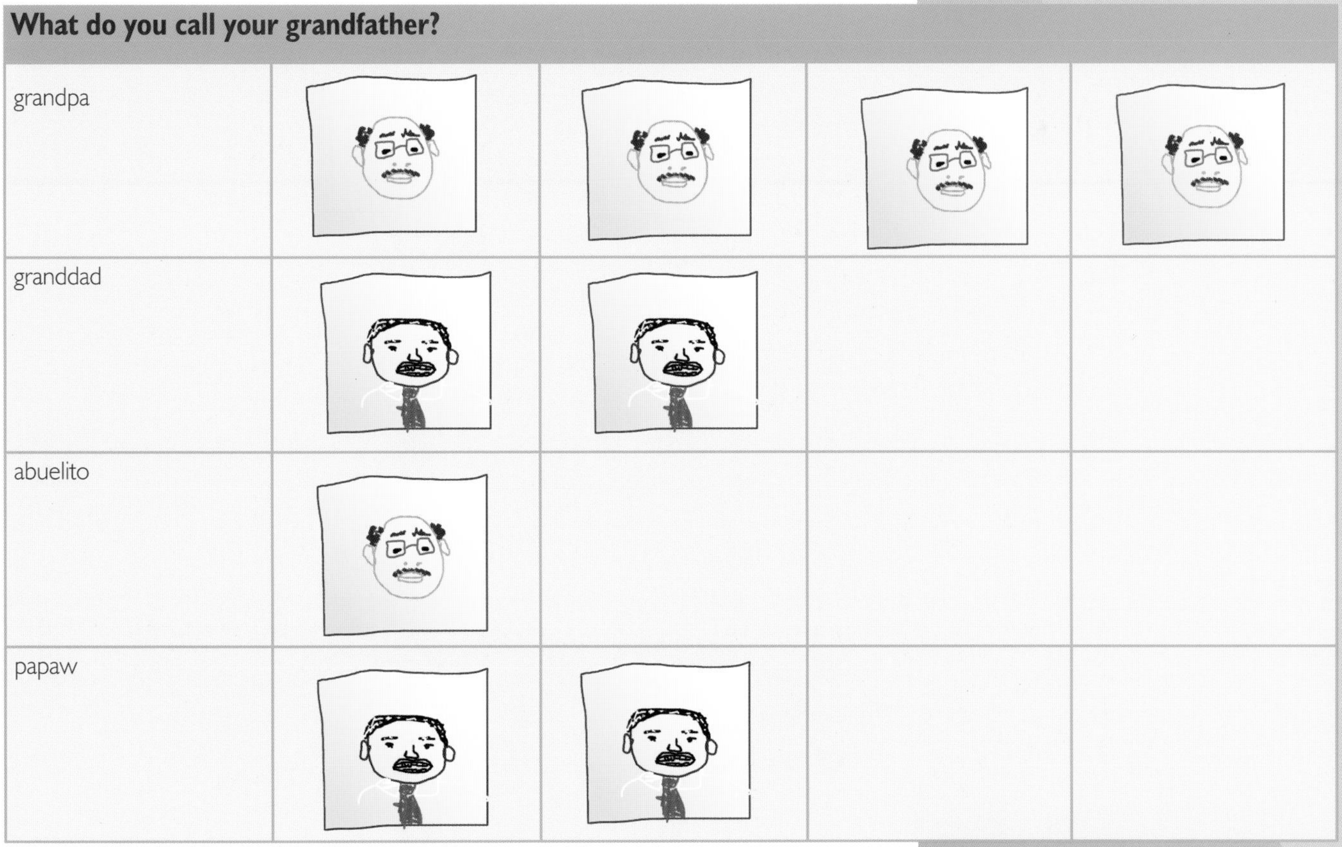

What's Needed
the book, *I Love Saturdays y domingos*
chart paper
markers
sticky notes or small pieces of paper

Social Studies Standards
Individual Development and Identity
O Exploring, identifying, and analyzing how individuals relate to one another

Individuals, Groups, and Institutions
O Understanding family structures and roles

Culture
O Exploring the cultures represented by the families in the classroom and community

What do you call your grandfather?

grandpa				
granddad				
abuelito				
papaw				

3. Have each child draw his grandfather's face on a sticky note and place it next to the name he uses. If four children call their grandfather "grandpa," there will be four sticky notes lined up next to that name on your pictograph (See the Birthday Pictograph on page 29 of this book for more information.).

4. Explain that a graph is a tool. We read it and get information from it. Look at the complete pictograph together and ask:

   What can we tell just by looking at our pictograph?
   What name is used most?

5. On another day, make a pictograph called "What do you call your grandmother?"

Talk with Children

Encourage children to discuss why there might be so many grandparent names.

Point out similarities and differences. You might say:

Harald calls his grandfather "Grandpa" and Elijah calls his "Gramp."
You and Logan both call your grandmother "Noni."

Think about the roles of grandparents. Ask:

What do you like to do with your grandparents?
How are grandparents different from parents?

Observe Children

Watch and listen to children as they work and document their understanding of the key objectives.

O Do the children listen to each other?
O As they fill in the graph, do they understand what it represents?
O Are the children clear about the relationships in their family?
O Do they understand that grandparents are their parents' parents?

EXTEND THE LEARNING

Have the children look at the breakfast food pages in *I Love Saturdays y domingos*.

Point out that Grandma makes spongy pancakes with honey and Abuelita makes huevos rancheros. Discuss different kinds of special foods the children's grandparents may make or serve. Record each child's contributions on chart paper. For example:

Carmela's Papa Pedro makes enchiladas.
Mei's Pop-Pop makes French fries.
Sacha's Gramp makes tomato sandwiches.

Have the children draw pictures on the chart to show the special foods.

Invite grandparents to bring samples of their special foods to share with the children.

CONNECT WITH FAMILIES

Display *I Love Saturdays y domingos* along with the "What do you call your grandfather (grandmother)?" pictographs. Post the following message to parents:

What's in a Name?

When we read *I Love Saturdays y domingos* we noticed that the little girl has special names for each of her grandparents. We made pictographs of the names we use for our grandfathers and our grandmothers.

We learned that:
- Grandparents are our parents' parents,
- Families often have special names for grandparents,
- All of our families have similarities, and
- All of our families are different.

See page 182 for a reproducible copy of this note to families.

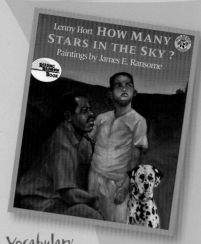

Vocabulary

Big Dipper: the seven brightest stars in the constellation Ursa Major

Jupiter: the largest planet in the solar system, fifth in order from the Sun

light pollution: excessive artificial light, especially street lighting in towns and cities, that prevents people from seeing the night sky clearly

Milky Way: a broad luminous irregular band of light that stretches completely around the celestial sphere and is caused by the light of myriads of faint stars

Social Studies Standards

Individual Development and Identity

- Describing characteristics of self
- Observing and trying to understand the behavior of siblings, peers, and adults

Book Talk

One night, while his mother is at work, a boy takes a ride with his father and shares a special time when they travel through towns, cities, and the countryside in order to count the stars.

MAKING CONNECTIONS

Before reading the book, talk with the children about special things they do with one or both of their parents. Is there one special thing they do with their mothers that they might not do with their fathers, or vice versa?

Invite the children to share their experiences about going out to look at the night sky. Did they see the moon and the stars? What else did they see in the sky?

INTRODUCING THE BOOK

Together, look at the cover of the book. Point to the words in the title as you read them aloud. Then, ask:

What do you think is the relationship between the people on the cover?
How do you think the boy is feeling in this picture?

Turn to the dedication page. Can the children identify the moon and stars in the sky? Can they count the stars?

READING AND TALKING TOGETHER

- Talk about the picture on the first page of the story. Explain that the boy can't go to sleep. Read the story aloud to find out what he does that night.
- Pause as you read to have the children talk about the pictures and discuss the place the boy and his father go to count stars. Talk about where they see the most stars and why.
- Ask the children to describe a time when they did something or went somewhere special with a grown-up. Ask:

What do you remember?
Where did you go?
What did you see?

SOCIAL STUDIES AND ME!

EXPLORATION:

MEMORY BOX

Each child will fill a traveling Memory Box with a small collection of items that are important to her. Children will share their Memory Boxes at group time.

What's Needed

5 small boxes
decorative paper
tape
collections of objects from home

Social Studies Standards

Individual Development and Identity

O Describing characteristics of self

O Observing and trying to understand the behavior of siblings, peers, and adults

Culture

O Understanding themselves both as individuals and as members of various groups

THINGS TO CONSIDER

This exploration requires children to bring things from home, so you will need to prepare well in advance. Send a note to parents explaining what you need for the Memory Box and when you would like to have it returned.

Send three or four boxes home at a time to ensure that there are always a couple of boxes that have been returned and are ready to be shared. If there are several boxes "out" and several boxes "in" at all times, no one child is on the spot if his family has not returned the box yet. It will also give you time to help families who are having difficulty with the assignment.

Some children may have fewer possessions or mementos to share. Make sure this does not become a way to distinguish between children whose families have many economic resources and those who have fewer.

STEP BY STEP

1. In advance, cover five small boxes with decorative paper. Write the words "Memory Box" on each. Fill one box with your own personal mementoes.
2. Talk with the children about how people collect objects to remind them of special times or trips they've taken. Tell them they will have the opportunity to collect special items from home to put into a Memory Box.
3. Share your Memory Box with the children. Tell them about each object. Then, write your name at the top of a chart. List your favorite object and why it's important to you. Display your box and the chart where families can see it, with a prominent sign, "Ms. Martin's Memory Box."
4. Send a note home asking families to help their child select a small collection of items (up to five) that are important to them. Explain that the Memory Box will help children learn special things about each other.
5. When a child returns with a filled box, let her share it with the group. As the child talks about and passes around the items, encourage other children to ask questions about where the item came from, who gave it to the child, and why it is special.

6. As each child shares his box, add information to the chart.

Name	Object	Why it is important to me
Ms. Keene	lava rock	found it by a volcano
Bobby	quartz crystal	Grandma gave it to me
Lilly	picture of me and Joe	we are good friends

Talk with Children

One rich part of this exploration is the stories that children tell about their box items. Prompt children to describe the events: *Your big brother gave you that award. What is the story about winning the award?*

Often a photograph is in the box. Say: *Tell us about the people in this photograph. What makes them special?*

Some children may not want to speak in front of the group. Have their families tell you the stories behind the items in the Memory Box so you can share them, or have a family member join you for the activity and answer questions for the class.

SOCIAL STUDIES AND ME!

Observe Children

- Do the children share objects, pass them around, and talk about them?
- Do the children ask and answer questions?
- Are topics for further study emerging, such as pets, siblings, or vacations?

EXTEND THE LEARNING

Use this exploration as an opportunity to learn more about characters in books. Read another book to the children from *Social Studies and Me!* (you might want to try *Cleversticks* or *Down the Road*). Ask them:

Who is this book about?

What might that character put in a Memory Box? Why?

Some children may want to start a new Memory Box at home. You might ask periodically:

Does anyone have anything new in their Memory Box? Tell me about the time (person, place) it helps you remember.

CONNECT WITH FAMILIES

Families will be working with you to select objects for the Memory Box. Try to give each family an individual report on how their child presented the box, the descriptive words used, and how comfortable the child seemed to be talking to the group.

When all children have had a chance to share their Memory Boxes, display the chart you made with an explanation:

Memory Box

Thank you for helping us put together our Memory Boxes. Here is a chart showing the things that are special to the children because they help bring back memories of special times, events, or people. In making and sharing Memory Boxes, we:

- Learned about ourselves as individuals and as parts of groups,
- Increased our understanding of each other, and
- Described our own characteristics, especially what we like and care about.

See page 183 for a reproducible copy of this note to families.

What's Needed

toy animals, people, and vehicles
variety of boxes
variety of art scraps
glue, tape
scissors
paint and paintbrushes

Social Studies Standards

People, Places, and Environments

o To draw upon immediate personal experiences as a basis for exploring geographic concepts and skills

o To think about similarities and differences between our own environments and other locations

EXPLORATION:

CREATE WHERE YOU LIVE

Children will use blocks, cardboard, modeling clay, and other assorted materials to create a three-dimensional model of a town, city or countryside. They will populate the community with toy animals or people and other materials.

THINGS TO CONSIDER

The goal of this exploration is not to create an exact replica of an actual place, but to create features that make a town, city, or countryside distinctive.

Guide the children to look closely at the pictures in the book *How Many Stars in the Sky?* for clues about the landscapes in each of the environments, and then encourage creativity as they work with common art materials and discarded pieces to create the features of towns, cities, and rural areas.

STEP BY STEP

1. With your group, study the pictures in *How Many Stars in the Sky?* Talk about the different locations you see in the book. Ask:

   What things do you see in a city?
   How is the city different from the country?
   What sounds might you hear in the country?
   What sounds might you hear in the city?
   How are buildings in a city different from the buildings in the country?
   How is a small town or village the same as and how is it different from both the city and the country?

2. Ask the children to choose (or vote for) an environment they would like to create together.
3. Using available materials, stack, cut, paint, glue, and tape to construct a city, town, or countryside. Use toy animals or people to populate it.
4. Leave this center open and available for free play.

Talk with Children

Building projects provide excellent opportunities for discussion. You might say:

Tell me about this skyscraper. How can we make it taller and sturdier?
This cereal box will be a perfect house. What will you use to build the barn?
Where will you put the library?

SOCIAL STUDIES AND ME!

Observe Children

○ Listen to hear if children are talking about the purpose of their structures as they build.

○ Notice if children are interested in creating the environment in which they live, or one they have visited, imagined, read, or talked about.

○ Observe and make notes about how well individual children work with others during this project.

EXTEND THE LEARNING

Once the children have created the town, city, or countryside, talk with them about who lives in that environment. Refer back to discussions you have had about transportation and careers. Ask:

What are some of the jobs people do in the city?

How do people travel in a city?

How do children get to school in the country?

How do farmers get their crops to the city?

Invite the children to add toy vehicles to their model environments.

CONNECT WITH FAMILIES

Set up a display area in a place visible to families. Display *How Many Stars in the Sky?* and your construction project. Label your project to indicate the environment. Post a note that says:

Create Your Own Environment

The book *How Many Stars in the Sky?* introduced children to the concepts of city, town, and countryside. We decided to learn more about _____ (insert whichever environment children created) and have created this model to show what it might look like. What features do you notice that show you the children have learned a lot about this particular place?

See page 183 for a reproducible copy of this note to families.

Down the Road

Alice Schertle

ILLUSTRATED BY *E.B. Lewis*

BOOK TALK

Hetty wants to prove to her parents that she's old enough to go to the old country store by herself. She goes down the dirt road to pick up a dozen eggs. She is very careful not to break them on her way home, but she runs into trouble when she stops to pick apples.

This story is about independence, making choices, taking risks, and the comfort of a family's love and forgiveness.

Vocabulary

clutter: a mess

dillydally: to waste time by being too slow

nudge: to push or move gently

Social Studies Standards

Individual Development and Identity

○ Exploring, identifying, and analyzing how individuals relate to one another

Civic Ideals and Practices

○ Understanding cause and effect and how they relate to personal experiences

Production, Distribution, and Consumption

○ Observing, discussing, and dramatizing basic economic concepts such as buying and selling and producing and consuming

MAKING CONNECTIONS

Before reading *Down the Road* with your group, engage the children in a discussion about feelings and how they can change. Ask: *What are some things that make you feel sad, happy, angry, embarrassed? What can happen to make your feelings change?*

Share a personal story with the children about a time you were sad. Explain why you were sad and what made the sadness go away. Invite volunteers to share their own experiences with the group.

INTRODUCING THE BOOK

Show the children the cover of *Down the Road*. Read the title of the book together. Ask: *What do you think the girl is doing in the picture?*

Share the art on the back cover. Talk about how the girl is carrying the eggs. Have children walk, carrying baskets on their heads, to help them understand how difficult it is.

Look at the title page together. Ask: *Where do you think this story takes place? What do you see that makes you think so? Where would the artist have to be to see the farm this way?*

READING AND TALKING TOGETHER

○ Explain that this book is about a little girl named Hetty, who goes down the road to get fresh eggs for her family. Let the children predict what will happen when she tries to carry the eggs home. Then, read aloud the story to find out.

○ After reading the book discuss Hetty's feelings. Ask:
How did Hetty feel when her parents let her walk to the store by herself?
How did she feel carrying the eggs?
How did she feel when the eggs broke?
How did she feel after she talked to her father?

○ Hetty feels grown-up because she's allowed to go down the road by herself and she has money in her pocket. Ask:
What are some of the things that make you feel grown-up?
What are some things that grown-ups do that children cannot do yet?
What are some of the things children do that grown-ups cannot do?

SOCIAL STUDIES AND ME!

EXPLORATION:

MY FAMILY MAP

Children think about who is in their family and create a "family map."

THINGS TO CONSIDER

This exploration will take a while to complete, as children will require individual attention.

Children live in various kinds of family structures; therefore they will be making many different kinds of family maps. Some children may need to put themselves on more than one family map to fully describe their family.

When drawing in front of the group in the first steps, it is best to draw very simple pictures so the children are not discouraged about their own developing drawing skills. You might say something like, *I'll use red to make a circle for an apple.* Or, *I'll draw a green triangle to make a dress for my Mom.*

STEP BY STEP

1. Ask: *Who is in Hetty's family? Tell me something about the people in Hetty's family.* You may need to do a picture walk through the book or reread sections of *Down the Road* to help the children remember details.

2. As children are talking, sketch a "map" of Hetty's family. Use the "Map of My Family" in *My Map Book* as a template. Write and draw Mama and Papa attached with a horizontal line. Add Hetty below and attach with a vertical line. Draw small details to stand for what children say about the character. (Apples near everyone because they like them, a car near Papa because he fixes cars, and so on.)

3. Think about what constitutes a family. You might say:

   Hetty's family is Mama and Papa and Hetty. What is a family? Guide the children to a definition of family wider than two parents and a child.

4. Explain that each child will be making a Family Map. Work with the children independently or in small groups to make their maps. Younger children can tell about who is in their family, while you sketch what they say onto their Family Map. Older children will be able to draw pictures but may need assistance writing the words and drawing the connecting lines between family members.

5. Have a few children share their Family Maps at group time each day.

Talk with Children

Listen to the children's comments. How do they communicate what they know about family? You can write their comments on a piece of chart paper as they seek to define family. You might ask:

What is a family?

What do people in a family do?

Who are the people in your family?

Observe Children

Notice if the children are comfortable talking about their families.

○ Are the children clear about the relationships in their families?

○ Do they know, for example, that Grandpa is Mom's father?

○ Do the children recognize similarities and differences between families?

○ Do the children enjoy making Family Maps and talking about their own families?

EXTEND THE LEARNING

At circle time, encourage the children to explore the question, *Are we a family here at school?* Refer to the comments children made previously to determine why or why not.

CONNECT WITH FAMILIES

Celebrate with families the learning that has taken place. Display *Down the Road* with children's Family Maps. Post a description of the exploration.

My Family Map

We are learning about families. We all dictated or drew maps of our families.

We learned:

▢ Families are people who love you,

▢ Families take care of each other,

▢ We all have families, and

▢ Families are all different.

See page 184 for a reproducible copy of this note to families.

EXPLORATION:

UNDERSTANDING EMOTIONS

Children identify different emotions and relate them to *Down the Road* and to their own lives.

What's Needed

set of cards that show different emotions
old magazines

Social Studies Standards

Individual Development and Identity
- Describing characteristics of self
- Observing and learning about the behavior of siblings, peers and adults
- Comparing patterns of behavior evident in age and ability

THINGS TO CONSIDER

In advance, collect cards, photographs, or pictures from magazines that show a variety of situations and emotions such as:

- Adults encouraging children and adults correcting children,
- Families doing things together and being happy,
- Children alone and sad,
- Happy children, and
- Children discouraged over a failure.

Read through the entire exploration and think about how you might discuss the cards or photographs. If while doing the exploration you notice that a child is especially sad or angry, you may want to discuss this with the child's family.

STEP BY STEP

1. Compare different moments in *Down the Road*. Ask:
   How does Hetty feel when her father says she can go to the store by herself?
   How does she feel when he finds her in the tree?

2. Share the emotion cards or photographs that show adults encouraging children and adults correcting children. For each picture, ask:
   What is happening here?
   Why do you think they are acting this way?
   What is each person feeling?
   Let's make up a story about what is going on.

3. Look at the final scene in *Down the Road* when the whole family is eating pie, and compare it to Hetty sitting all alone in the tree. What is the same? What is different? Share cards or photographs showing families together and happy or children alone and sad. For each picture, ask:
   What is happening here?
   Why do you think they are acting this way?
   What is each person feeling?
   Let's make up a story about what is going on here.

4. Share cards or photos of children achieving something and being happy, or children discouraged over a failure. Ask questions such as these:
   How would you feel?
   Does Hetty ever feel this way?

Talk with Children

Some children will understand the emotions depicted and use them dramatically or in story form, while others will stop at simple, one-word labels. Start with basic emotion words as you interact with children. Ask: *Does this boy look happy? Sad? Mad? Hurt? Afraid? Ashamed?*

Help to extend their emotions vocabulary. Say:
This boy seems sad. He seems upset. He looks like he wants to cry.
This girl looks happy. She looks delighted. She looks satisfied.
This boy seems mad. He looks angry. He seems fierce.

Observe Children

○ What are you learning about the children from this exploration? Are they comfortable expressing feelings of pride and achievement? Are they comfortable talking about times when their parents are mad at them or proud of them?

○ If it seems as though a child is especially sad or angry you may want to discuss your concerns with the family. You should also familiarize yourself with mental health resources for children in your community so you can respond to any extreme situations that you observe.

EXTEND THE LEARNING

Make a Big Book of Emotions. Invite the children to tell you about times when they feel sad, happy, proud, angry, loving, or any other feelings.

Write this sentence frame on each page of the book.
(Name of child) feels (list emotion) when (list what the child says).

Help each child come up with three examples of feelings and what makes her feel that way. Then let the children illustrate or decorate the pages of the big book. Read the completed Big Book of Emotions to the group.

CONNECT WITH FAMILIES

Display *Down the Road* with a sample of the emotion cards or photographs you've collected. If your group made a Big Book of Emotions, display it and post the following:

Understanding Emotions

We read *Down the Road* together and saw how the characters felt at different times during the story. We have been talking about feelings, naming them, and sharing about what makes us feel one way or another. When we did this we learned:

▢ To describe some of our own feelings,

▢ To notice that people behave differently at different ages,

▢ To observe the feelings and behavior of our siblings, our peers, and of adults, and

▢ To recognize and explore similarities and differences among individuals' and groups' beliefs and feelings.

See page 184 for a reproducible copy of this note to families.

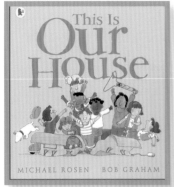

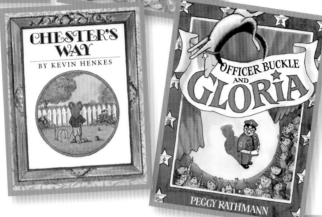

This Is Our House
by Michael Rosen
Illustrated by Bob Graham

Chester's Way
by Kevin Henkes

Jamaica and Brianna
by Juanita Havill
Illustrated by Anne Sibley O'Brien

Officer Buckle and Gloria
by Peggy Rathmann

CHAPTER 4

Friends

INTRODUCING THE THEME

SPARKING CURIOSITY

Friendship is very important to young children. Think how often we hear children say things such as, *I'll be your best friend,* or *Will you be my friend?*

Young children enjoy playing with each other and they are very interested in having friends. As this interest grows, children want to explore and experience many different friendships. They enjoy making friends, talking with friends, playing with friends, helping friends, and laughing with friends.

Books about different kinds of relationships appeal to young children. They not only enjoy the stories, but they can also begin to learn lessons about relationships from such books. These lessons about friendship are an important part of social studies in the early years.

For young children, friendship is a puzzle with many pieces. Children are learning that:

○ Friends know each other's names,
○ Friends are polite and kind to each other,
○ Friends enjoy talking and listening to each other,
○ Friends help each other,
○ Friends share and take turns,
○ Friends solve problems by talking together,
○ Friends can be quite different from each other,
○ Friends notice things about each other,
○ Friends enjoy jokes, silliness, and laughing, and
○ Friends remember and plan together.

BUILDING BACKGROUND

Learning to be a good friend, playmate, and classmate does not happen quickly. Coaching from patient adults, learning from mistakes, and reading good books about social relationships all help young children grow increasingly more skilled at making and keeping friends.

A teacher cannot make friends for a child, but she can give him the tools to use to build friendship skills. To support the development of friendships, try some of these strategies:

○ Offer a variety of opportunities for children to interact.
○ Model how to talk and play with others.
○ Teach and model empathy.
○ Point out children's strengths and encourage them to feel good about themselves and each other.
○ Remind children to smile, wave, speak to others, and initiate play.

Some ideas to start you thinking about social studies:

Idea

When we remember that social studies is about how people live in our society, it is easy to understand the significance of the role of friends. As you grow familiar with the standards, you will see that thinking and talking about friends and working on social skills touches nearly every aspect of social studies.

SOCIAL STUDIES AND ME!

Some ideas to start you thinking about language and literacy:

Idea   While some children seem to learn how to talk with their friends effortlessly, others may need coaching and reminders to learn the talking skills that friendship requires. Teach children to use language like:

Jessie, I like your picture because...
Vanessa, can I have a turn after you?
Sam, I don't like it when you...

Poem:

Girls and boys, come out to play,
The moon does shine as bright as day.
Leave your supper and leave your sleep,
And come with your friends out into the street.
Come with a whoop! Come with a call!
Come with goodwill or don't come at all!
Up the ladder and down the wall,
A halfpenny roll will serve us all.
You find milk, and I'll find flour,
And we'll have a pudding in half an hour.
                                    —*Traditional*

The poems included in this book are simple and very accessible to young children. Look for collections of Mother Goose rhymes in your local library.

This Is
Our
House

MICHAEL ROSEN   BOB GRAHAM

Vocabulary

bookplate: a label to put in the front of a book, bearing the name of the owner and sometimes a coat of arms or personal design

bully: someone who uses words or her body to threaten or scare someone else

rescue: to save someone

share: to allow somebody to use something or have part of something

Social Studies Standards

Individual Development and Identity

○ Comparing how we are similar to and different from others

Power, Authority, and Governance

○ Exploring fairness in our relationships with others

○ Understanding how individuals and groups work to resolve conflicts

BOOK TALK

George has a cardboard house. He says that the house is HIS and no one else can play in it because they are different from him—they have glasses, they are twins, they are small. When George comes back from a trip to the bathroom, he finds he is the odd man out. The children help George understand that it's more fun when the house is for EVERYONE.

MAKING CONNECTIONS

This Is Our House is a book about sharing resources, sharing space, and making rules. It's also about inclusion and exclusion. Before you read the book with the children, talk with them about being bossy. You might ask these questions: *What does it mean to be bossy? Has anyone here ever been bossy? What does it feel like to be bossed around?*

INTRODUCING THE BOOK

Before you read the book *This Is Our House*, read the names of the author and the illustrator. Look at the art on the covers and ask: *What are the children doing? Do you think they know each other? Why or why not? Why do you think the title of the book is "This Is Our House?"*

Before the endpapers in this book (the first and last full-page spreads) there is a page with a blank bookplate. Ask the children if they have bookplates in any of their books at home. If this is a class book, you might fill in the bookplate with the name of your class.

Look at the endpapers. Ask: *Where does this story take place? How do the endpapers at the beginning look different from those at the back?*

READING AND TALKING TOGETHER

○ Ask the children why they think the title of the book is *This Is Our House*. After your discussion, read the book to find out.

○ After reading the book, talk about George's behavior. Ask:
   Why do you think he wouldn't let anyone else play in the cardboard house?
   How do you think the other children felt?
   Tell about a time you felt left out.
   Why do you think George is treating his friends like this?

○ Discuss what happens when George comes back from the bathroom. Ask: *How did George feel when he was left out? How did he show what he felt?*
   George liked being alone IN the house, but not about being alone OUTSIDE the house. *Why do you think that is so? How did George make it work out for everyone?*

○ Talk about how the illustrator uses color only with the characters who are directly involved on that page, while other characters are drawn in gray. You will also notice that the artist has used frames to highlight the action.

SOCIAL STUDIES AND ME!

EXPLORATION:

THIS CLASSROOM IS FOR EVERYONE!

Children discuss the rules George made in *This Is Our House* and rules that they themselves must abide by. Do the rules seem fair or unfair? Is there a rule that they would want changed? How could they change it? After discussion, the children develop a list of rules for the classroom.

THINGS TO CONSIDER

This exploration involves a lot of talking, listening, and thinking about rules. You will need to spread it over a few days.

Think carefully about your classroom rules. Strive to keep an open mind as children express their opinions. They may say that a rule such as, "only four children allowed in the block area" is unfair. Consider why the rule exists. Can or should it be changed?

This exploration helps children understand that there is more than one point of view when it comes to rules. Is every child developmentally ready to understand another person's point of view? Be prepared to keep the conversation simple and concrete.

STEP BY STEP

1. Reread *This Is Our House.* Pause to point out the rules George had for the house. Ask: *What do you think about George's rules?*
2. Look at the last page of the book where all of the characters agree that the rule should be, "This house is for everyone." Say: *This book made me think about rules and what makes them fair.*
3. Together, brainstorm a list of school rules. Read through the list and ask:
   Why do we have this rule?
   Do you think it is fair? Why or why not?
4. Ask the children to vote on whether they think each rule is fair or not fair and to stand by the appropriate sign: FAIR or NOT FAIR. As the children vote, point out that people have different opinions about what's fair.
5. Display a chart with "This Classroom Is for Everyone!" written across the top and say: *I will write the rules we all agree on.* Help the children shape the rules into positive sentences. They may say things like, "no hitting" and then "no pinching, no pushing." Those rules could be restated as "Use words instead of hands," or "Gentle touches only".
6. When you have a list everyone agrees on, the children can sign their names on the bottom to make it official. Hang the list where the children can see it and refer to it often.

What's Needed

the book, *This Is Our House*
chart paper
markers
two teacher-made signs: FAIR and
  UNFAIR

Social Studies Standards

Civic Ideals and Practices
O Understanding balance between rights and responsibilities

Power, Authority, and Governance
O Exploring fairness in their relationships with others
O Understanding and making classroom rules
O Understanding that there can be different rules in different contexts

Talk with Children

Were there any classroom rules that many children voted UNFAIR? Can the children think of how they might be changed? Be sure to use the language of logic, or cause and effect in this discussion. For example:

The rule is, "Do not throw snowballs," because someone might get hurt. The woods next to the playground have no people in them. If we throw snowballs into the woods, then nobody will get hurt. So the new rule is, "Throw snowballs over the fence into the woods."

Help the children hear each other's ideas by repeating their words:

Jake says we need a rule, "No walking with scissors." Salehe says sometimes we need to carry scissors from the art shelf to the work table. What should we do?

Observe Children

Observe and document the children's behaviors and points of view.

O Do the children have strong opinions about George's rules? Classroom rules? What are their opinions?

O Are there children who don't know any classroom rules? Why haven't they become aware of them?

O Pay attention to how the children use the vocabulary of this exploration. Do they need some extra support with concepts such as: if…then, now…later, before… after, why…because? Without an understanding of these terms, life can seem very unfair.

O Do the children refer to the posted rules in their play?

O Try to notice the children following the rules so you can point it out to them:
Hannah, I see that you are making room for Louise. You are remembering the rule, "We share toys at school."

EXTEND THE LEARNING

Write the rules on smaller paper and photocopy this list for the children. They can decorate the edges of the paper (like a frame) and hang it up somewhere in their home.

Ask the children to create a list of fair rules to guide conduct in the local community. For example: "When you are at the movie theater, you must be very quiet so others can hear the movie, too." Another might be: "Don't cut in line. Everyone has to wait his turn."

CONNECT WITH FAMILIES

Create a bulletin board display to share your work with families. Display *This Is Our House* and the This Classroom Is for Everyone! chart. Add this note:

This Classroom Is for Everyone!

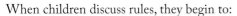

In *This Is Our House,* George made very unfair rules. The other children worked to create a rule that was fair to all. We discussed some of our classroom rules and have voted on which rules we think are fair or not fair. We made a list of classroom rules we all agree to follow.

See page 185 for a reproducible copy of this note to families.

When children discuss rules, they begin to:

○ Learn about the needs and wants of other people,

○ Understand some of the ways people in communities, families and schools work together to get along,

○ Learn about balancing the needs of individuals and the needs of the group,

○ Understand that rules help keep us safe, and

○ Learn that there can be different rules for different situations (classroom, home, indoors, outdoors, and so on).

What's Needed

chart paper
materials for building museum
    walls
materials for building display cases
signs
objects to display

Social Studies Standards

Individual Development and Identity

○ Exploring, identifying, and analyzing how individuals relate to one another

Civic Ideals and Practices

○ Understanding how an individual can make a positive difference in the community

○ Determining how to balance the needs of individuals with the needs of the group

EXPLORATION:

THIS IS OUR CLASSROOM MUSEUM

In this exploration, the children plan, design, and build a classroom museum.

THINGS TO CONSIDER

Has your group ever visited a museum? If your community has a museum, historic building, or nature center, take the children on a field trip.

This project will take several days to complete. Schedule a little time each day to work on it.

STEP BY STEP

1. Explain that a museum is a place where collections of objects are stored and displayed for everyone to see and learn about. Ask:

   Have you ever visited a museum?
   What kind of museum was it?
   What did you see?
   What did you learn from your visit to the museum?

As the children talk, make a list of the museums they have visited.

2. Work together to build a classroom museum. First, brainstorm a list of ideas for the museum (collections of rocks, toys, buttons, or any objects that can be displayed easily). Steer the discussion towards a choice of objects all the children will have access to. Have the children vote on what kind of museum they'll construct, and decide how you will go about collecting the objects for display.

3. Make a list of the jobs required to build the museum and the materials you will need. A sample list is shown.

build the museum	bookshelves
construct the exhibits	boxes, trays, magnifying glass, tweezers
organize the objects in each display	rocks, fossils, shells, bones
label the objects	paper, crayons, scissors, tape

4. Decide who will do each job. Work in cooperative groups to make the museum. When it is complete, invite families to visit with their children.

Talk with Children

Remind the children how important it is that they work together and cooperate as they plan and build. Ask leading questions and make comments about all the tasks they're doing. For example:

How can you show all of these different rocks?

How can we choose which ones to display in this space?

What materials do the three of you think you'll need to build the walls of the museum?

Talk with the children about what visitors will learn from their museum.

Observe Children

Observe the children and make notes about their work.

○ Do the children who've already visited museums share their experiences with other children?

○ Are some children more apt to work alone than in teams?

○ How can you encourage those children to work with other children?

EXTEND THE LEARNING

Follow up by inviting a museum educator to visit your classroom. Set some goals for the visit and tell the educator about your classroom museum and what the children have learned during the exploration.

CONNECT WITH FAMILIES

Invite families to visit the classroom museum. Have children take turns giving tours of the museum displays. Display *This Is Our House*, along with the following:

This Is Our Classroom Museum

After we read *This Is Our House*, we decided to work together to build a classroom museum. We collaborated on planning, designing, and building our museum. We learned about:

- ▫ Cooperation,
- ▫ Needs and wants, and
- ▫ Making choices.

See page 185 for a reproducible copy of this note to families.

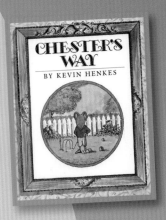

CHESTER'S WAY
BY KEVIN HENKES

Friends

Kevin Henkes explores how people can open themselves up to new experiences, and how having new friends enriches your life.

Vocabulary

disguise: something worn or done to change somebody's appearance so others don't recognize the person

nifty: something clever, neat or excellent

"two peas in a pod": very much alike

Social Studies Standards

Individual Development and Identity

○ Comparing how we are similar to and different from others
○ Observing and learning to understand the behavior of siblings, peers and adults

Individuals, Groups, and Institutions

○ Exploring the interactions among and within various groups and institutions

BOOK TALK

Chester knows what he likes and how he likes to have things done. His friend Wilson is just the same. Chester and Wilson were inseparable. And then Lily, a girl with a completely different style, moves into the neighborhood. How can people who are so different become friends?

MAKING CONNECTIONS

Talk with the children about friends. You might ask:

What is a friend?
What makes a friend special?
What are some things you do with your friend?
How are you like your best friend?

Talk with the children about the "friends" list on page 80 of this book.

INTRODUCING THE BOOK

Hold up the book and examine the cover together. The book is called *Chester's Way.* Ask:

Who do you think this might be on the cover?
What does it look like Chester is doing?

Invite children who have played croquet to share their experiences.

Explain that Chester has a special way of doing things. Flip through the pages, looking for pictures that show how Chester does things. Then, read the book to discover what Chester's way is.

READING AND TALKING TOGETHER

○ Read the story all the way through the first time. This is a story with a lot of suspense and tension.
○ After reading the book again, look at and talk about the illustrations. Ask:
    How are Chester and Wilson alike?
    How is Lily different from Chester and Wilson?
    What does it mean to "have a mind of your own"?
    What special things do you do when you have a mind of your own?
○ Chester and Wilson teach Lily new things and she teaches them new things. Talk about how we learn from our friends. Ask:
    Can you describe something you learned from a friend?
    Did you ever teach a friend to do something new? What was it?

SOCIAL STUDIES AND ME!

EXPLORATION:

MAKING FRIENDS AND KEEPING THEM

During this exploration, the children focus on friendship behaviors: how friends act, what friends say, and how friends feel about each other.

What's Needed

emotions cards
photographs of friends playing
pictures of children in need of companionship

Social Studies Standards

Individual Development and Identity

o Observing and learning to understand the behavior of siblings, peers and adults
o Exploring, identifying and analyzing how individuals relate to one another

THINGS TO CONSIDER

Some children understand more clearly about how to make friends than others do. Reread the "friends" list on page 80. This will help you guide the children as they explore friendship.

STEP BY STEP

1. Begin this exploration with a discussion about friends. Ask:

   What are some special things about friends?
   Tell about a time someone was a friend to you.
   How have you been a friend to someone else?

2. One at a time, show the children the cards or photographs you've collected and have a discussion about each one. You might ask:

   What would you say if you wanted to play with these boys (girls)?
   If you were somewhere and you saw this happen, what would you do?
   What do you think this child might need from a friend?

3. Show a card that shows two or more children playing together. Invite the children in the class to play the roles of the children on the card. Suggest that you'd like to play with them. Model gestures, some things you could say, and what you could do to have them invite you to play. Smile, wave, and move toward them. Say things such as:

   Hi, my name is Susie.
   Can I play too?
   That looks like fun, can I have a turn?
   Do you need some help?
   Here, I can help.

4. Have the children act out other scenes from the cards or photos you collected. Have another child join them, using the phrases you have introduced.

Talk with Children

Use this exploration to teach a few basic social skills. You may need to practice a simple phrase like, "May I have a turn after you?" again and again to help some children learn not to grab or to take things without asking.

Observe Children

Notice which children enjoy doing dramatics. You may want to try other kinds of role playing and charades with them.

Listen to the children during free play. Children learn quickly. If they get results from using a new skill, they will continue to use that skill. Are they using new social skills? Are they receiving positive reinforcement from other children? Do you see children learning and applying new techniques for making friends?

EXTEND THE LEARNING

Make a classroom big book "What Do You Say When You Want To Play?" The frame for this book will be:

If someone is…	Then you can say…
Jumping	Can I jump too?
Crying	What is the matter?
Playing with a great toy	May I have a turn with that cool toy?

When every child has contributed an idea, the children can illustrate their pages in the book. Ask the children to dictate what they want you to write to caption their illustrations.

CONNECT WITH FAMILIES

Display *Chester's Way* and the cards or photographs you used in this exploration. Post the following note to families.

Making Friends and Keeping Them

In *Chester's Way*, Chester and Wilson are friends who do everything together. Then Lily moves into the neighborhood. Chester and Wilson learn that even though Lily does things differently, she is a true friend.

In this exploration we learned:

- Friends are special people,
- Friends help each other, and
- Friends do fun things together.

See page 186 for a reproducible copy of this note to families.

EXPLORATION:

I LIKE THIS, YOU LIKE THAT

Children will chart their likes and dislikes. They discover that like Chester, Wilson, and Lily, they each have their own likes and dislikes.

What's Needed
the book, *Chester's Way*
large pieces of drawing paper
markers
little sticky notes or linking cubes

Social Studies Standards
Individual Development and Identity
○ Comparing how we are similar to and different from others

Individuals, Groups, and Institutions
○ Exploring interactions among and within various groups

THINGS TO CONSIDER

Choose your graph questions and answers carefully. If you make a graph about colors, be sure to include brown and black as choices, as it is important that all colors are seen as valid favorites. If you make a graph about favorite foods, structure it carefully to avoid reinforcing stereotypes like "all children hate broccoli."

Once you start making graphs, the possibilities for data collection and representation are endless!

STEP BY STEP

1. After reading *Chester's Way*, lead a discussion about what Chester, Wilson, and Lily like and dislike. Do a picture walk through the book, perhaps rereading key sentences, to recall specific details. You might ask:
   What kinds of things do Chester and Wilson like?
   What does Lily like that is different?
   What new things do they learn to like when they become friends?

2. Make pictographs to show what the children in your class like and dislike. Begin with a "What's our favorite pizza topping?" graph, following the example shown on page 30 of this book. Explain that a graph is a way of sharing information. Tell them that when your graph is done, people will be able to tell, just by looking, which pizza topping is the most popular in your class.

3. Post the pictograph on the board and read the question. Say:
   Decide now in your mind how you will answer this question.
   Don't tell anyone because you will show us on the graph.

4. Have each child place a sticky note on the graph to indicate his favorite pizza topping. When all of the data is collected, ask:
   What can we tell by looking at this graph?

Note: This step is important because it demonstrates that a graph is a tool that we use. We "read" it and get information from it.

5. Depending on the size of your group, you may want to complete one graph each day over several days. Choose a different topic each day or connect the graphing to one of your daily activities.

Talk with Children

Encourage the children to use comparative language (more, less, same, most, least) to analyze the graph.

Most people like pepperoni best.

The same number of people like sausage and mushrooms best.

Four people like tomatoes best. Zero people like onions. Four is more than zero. So, more people like tomatoes than onions.

Observe Children

O Do the children notice that their friends have similar (or different) preferences?

O Are the children comfortable with these differences?

O Are the children able to read information from the graph?

O What words do the children use to express what they see on the graph?

EXTEND THE LEARNING

Put the same questions on new graphs for parents or caregivers to complete at drop-off or pick-up time. Compare the results from the graphs done by the children with the ones done by the adults.

CONNECT WITH FAMILIES

Make a bulletin board display to show the materials used and created in this exploration. Display *Chester's Way* with the completed graphs. Post the following:

I Like This, You Like That

After reading *Chester's Way* we made some graphs and discovered that, just like Chester, Wilson, and Lily, we each have our own likes and dislikes. We are unique individuals but we also share many of the same traits and interests.

We talked about how:

◘ We all like to do things our way,

◘ We can learn to like new things and new ways,

◘ Friends can like different things and still be friends,

◘ Friends can like similar things, and

◘ A graph can show us a lot of information.

See page 186 for a reproducible copy of this note to families.

BOOK TALK

Jamaica hates having to wear her brother's hand-me-down boots, especially when her friend Brianna teases her about them being "boy boots." When Jamaica gets to buy her own new pair, she chooses tan cowboy boots and tells Brianna that her pink fuzzy boots are ugly. How can they work things out?

MAKING CONNECTIONS

Hand-me-downs are common in many families with more than one child. Hand-me-downs are also passed from one family to another.

Talk about wearing hand-me-downs and how the children feel about it. Ask:
Do you ever wear something that someone else has worn before you?
How do you feel about that?
Talk about a time you went to a store to buy new clothes. Who chose the clothes?

Ask the children to tell about a piece of clothing another child is wearing that they particularly like. *You like Emma's shoes. What is it you like about them?*

INTRODUCING THE BOOK

Show the cover of the book *Jamaica and Brianna* and read the title. Point to each girl in the picture as you say her name. Ask the children:
What do you think this story will be about?
What do you notice about their boots? Are they the same or different?

Look at the title page and ask:
Can you tell from the picture how Jamaica feels about her boots?
What do you think she will do?
Have the children make predictions about the story. Then read to find out what happens.

READING AND TALKING TOGETHER

○ Read the story through. There is a lot of tension in the story that is happily resolved in the end.

○ Talk about how it feels when someone else has something that is newer, bigger, or fancier than yours. Introduce the word jealous into your discussion. Ask:
How does Jamaica feel about her boots?
How does she feel about Brianna's boots? Is she jealous?
Which do you think is more important, having fancy boots or having a friend?
Why do you think this?

Vocabulary
embarrassed: ashamed
fair: to share equally; to treat participants equally
scrunch: to crumple, crush, or squeeze something together tightly
slop: soft mud or slushy snow

Social Studies Standards
Individual Development and Identity
○ Understanding our own basic needs and wants and those of others

Power, Authority, and Governance
○ Understanding how individuals and groups work to resolve conflicts

○ *Jamaica and Brianna* hurt each other's feelings by what they say. Turn to the page where Brianna says "Cowboy boots aren't in." Ask:

How would you feel if someone said that to you?

Why do you think Jamaica says something mean back?

○ The friends talk through their misunderstanding. Talk about ways to tell someone when your feelings are hurt. Ask:

If someone says something that hurts your feelings, what could you say?

EXPLORATION:

I LIKE YOU BECAUSE...

Children will think about their friends and compose an "I like you because…." poem for a friend.

What's Needed
"I Like You Because…" poem
chart paper
markers

Social Studies Standards
Individual Development and Identity
- Comparing how we are similar to and different from others
- Understanding our own basic needs and wants and those of others
- Exploring, identifying, and analyzing how individuals relate to one another

THINGS TO CONSIDER

In advance, create your own "I like you because. . ." poem to share with the children. (See below.) Write it on chart paper. Be sure to include the title of the poem and the name of the poet (yourself!).

Children will need time to discuss their poem ideas with you and the group. You may want to spend extra time brainstorming ideas before the children begin writing.

STEP BY STEP

1. Talk about poems. Tell the children that a poet (the person who writes the poem) uses carefully chosen words to make a "word picture." Poets often make comparisons between different things. Here are some examples:

   As soft as a cotton ball
   As funny as a clown
   As beautiful as the moon
   Your face is like the sun
   Your voice is like a sparrow's song

2. After sharing those comparisons, engage the children in creating some comparisons of their own. Give the children plenty of practice making and completing comparisons. Begin with these:

   Your hair is curly, like _____.
   Your eyes are as blue as _____.
   Your feet are as loud as _____.

3. Read aloud your own "I like you because . . ." poem (see example).

4. Allow time for each child to think of someone in her family to write about in an "I like you because…." poem. Provide help and hints as needed. Encourage the children to help each other with descriptive words.

5. Make a class book of your poems. Each child's poem can be on one page with a drawing of her friend on the opposite page. A child may have an opinion of where the words should be placed on the page.

I like you because . . .
By Mrs. Becker
I like you because your hair is as red as the setting sun.
I like you because you make cookies that smell like honey.
I like you because you wrap me up in hugs.
I like you because you hop like a bunny.

Talk with Children

Invite the children to talk about their special friends and the reasons why they like them. Grandparents, siblings, neighbors, pets, and even toys may be good friends to young children. Give them some prompts, such as:

Can you tell me what Sarah likes to do?
Can you tell me about what Max looks like?
Can you tell me what games you and Juan play?
Where do you like to take your teddy bear?

If a child does not go beyond a phrase such as, "I like you because you are pretty," that is fine. Children need a lot of experience with this type of thinking and writing.

Observe Children

○ Listen for the new and interesting words children use.
○ Note which children are able to make long or rhyming sentences about their friends.
○ Can the children articulate what they like about others?

EXTEND THE LEARNING

Encourage the children to write "I like _____ because _____" poems about seasons, holidays, or other special occasions. For example:

I like summer because it's sunny and hot.
I like my birthday because my mom makes me a big cake.

Ask the children to illustrate the poems and make a poetry gallery in your classroom.

CONNECT WITH FAMILIES

Communicate with families often about the learning that is taking place in your classroom. Send home samples of the children's work. Invite them to look at the display for this exploration. Display *Jamaica and Brianna* with the children's poems, the classroom book of poetry, and the following:

I Like You Because...

We have been reading *Jamaica and Brianna*, a book about friends. We are continuing our exploration of friendship by writing poems. Each of us wrote a poem called, "I Like You Because…." about a friend. The poems were bound into a class book. Please ask to borrow this book so your family can enjoy reading it together. By thinking about friendship and writing poems about it we are learning:

▪ What characteristics we think are special,
▪ How we are the same and different, and
▪ To remember the past and imagine the future.

See page 187 for a reproducible copy of this note to families.

EXPLORATION:

IT'S A SHOE-IN!

In this exploration, children invent shoe designs to sell in a class "shoe store."

What's Needed
the book, *Jamaica and Brianna*
two small shoe boxes for each child
scissors and glue
paint and paintbrushes
feathers, sequins, glitter
art scraps
decorative paper

.

THINGS TO CONSIDER

In advance, turn the boxes into "shoes" by cutting a hole in the bottom of each. The holes should be just big enough for a child to slip a foot in.

Some children will have a clear plan in mind for their shoes. Others will be inspired by the materials and decorate them without a plan.

Children will have different experiences with shoe stores. Some will know stores that are self-serve with all the sizes on display. Others will have experience in stores with clerks who measure the customer's feet then get the shoes from the back room.

Social Studies Standards
Production, Distribution, and Consumption
- Understanding the difference between wants and needs and making decisions based on this understanding
- Observing, discussing, and dramatizing basic economic concepts such as buying and selling and producing and consuming
- Identifying and discussing the duties of a variety of community occupations

STEP BY STEP

1. Look back at the pictures in *Jamaica and Brianna.* Ask the children:
   What makes snow boots special for snow?
   Why are cowboy boots good for someone who works on a ranch?

2. Show the children the boxes and the art materials and explain that they are going to create special shoes for a shoe store. Ask the children what they might do with the materials, such as make flying shoes with wings, party shoes with glitter, or funny shoes with ears and a tail.

3. Model how you might design your shoes. Be sure to explain about not decorating the bottom of the shoes so they can really be worn. Encourage creativity.

4. When the shoes are dry and ready to wear, invite children to set up a shoe store in the classroom. Stock the shelves with all of the shoes the class designed.

5. Let the children have time for free play in the shoe store. They can try on shoes and take turns playing customer and sales person.

Talk with Children

Encourage the children to talk about the shoes they designed. Ask:
What are your shoes for?
What materials did you use?
Who might wear them?

Observe Children

○ How do the children create their shoes?

○ Do the materials inspire them, or do they start with a plan?

○ Do they see a connection between form and function?

○ Notice if the children understand the idea of buying and selling, and if they are using the language of shopping: buy, pay for, return, change, charge, and cost.

EXTEND THE LEARNING

As children begin to explore the shoe store, extend the exploration by saying:

Where will you display the shoes?

Where shall we put the cash register?

How will you ask her for the purple shoes?

I remember the last time I was in a store, a clerk said, "May I help you?"

Take the children on a field trip to a real shoe store. Ask a salesperson to show you how shoes are fitted to individual feet and to give you a tour of the store.

CONNECT WITH FAMILIES

Display *Jamaica and Brianna*, the shoes children designed, and if possible, photos of the children exploring their shoe store. Post the following to explain the exploration.

It's a Shoe-in!

After reading *Jamaica and Brianna* we became shoe designers. We talked about what we needed for our shoe designs, and then we created our shoes. When we were done we made a shoe store in the room and pretended to buy and sell our special shoes. We talked about:

◘ What special things we need for our shoes,

◘ How different kinds of shoes have special features,

◘ What a shoe store is like, and

◘ How to buy and sell things.

See page 187 for a reproducible copy of this note to families.

BOOK TALK

Officer Buckle gives safety talks at schools. His information is important, but no one is listening. When police dog Gloria goes with him, things take a surprising turn. Can Officer Buckle get over his disappointment when he finds out that it is his good friend Gloria who is making his talks so popular?

MAKING CONNECTIONS

Invite the children to share what they already know about police officers. Ask:

What do you think police officers do?

What else do you know about police officers?

What do they drive?

What special clothing and equipment do police officers have?

INTRODUCING THE BOOK

Together, look at the cover of the book *Officer Buckle and Gloria.* Who do the children think the book will be about?

Look at the inside covers of the book. Read some of the tips printed on the stars. What do the children already know about safety tips? Ask: *Can you think of any other safety tips?*

Flip through the pages of the book. Say: *Look for the places where Officer Buckle has posted his safety tips.*

READING AND TALKING TOGETHER

O Talk about what it means to work together as a team. Explain that in this story, Officer Buckle has the information and Gloria makes it fun to learn. Read the story aloud, pausing to look at the pictures and discuss what is happening.

O Ask questions about the story.
  What happens when Officer Buckle does his talk all by himself?
  What happens when Gloria tries to do it on her own?
  What happens in the end?

O Talk about experiences the children had when they worked on something together as a team. Ask:
  How did working together make the work better or more fun?

O Encourage discussions about how pets can be our friends, too. Begin by asking:
  Have you ever had a pet for a friend?
  What are some of the things you and your pet friend did together?

Vocabulary

enormous: unusually large or great in size, amount, or degree; huge. Other fun words for enormous are: gigantic, mammoth, colossal

police dog: a dog trained to work with the police

tip: a useful suggestion or idea for doing something

Social Studies Standards

Civic Ideals and Practices

O Understanding how an individual can make a positive difference in the community

Production, Distribution, and Consumption

O Identifying and discussing the duties of a variety of community occupations

Power, Authority, and Governance

O Understanding how individuals and groups work to resolve conflicts

What's Needed

chart paper
drawing paper
crayons
markers

Social Studies Standards

Civic Ideals and Practices

○ Understanding how an individual can make a positive difference in the community

Production, Distribution, and Consumption

○ Identifying and discussing the duties of a variety of community occupations

Power, Authority, and Governance

○ Understanding how individuals and groups work to resolve conflicts

EXPLORATION:

HOW DO YOU DO, OFFICER?

In this exploration, the children will meet a police officer. They will learn what it would be like to be a police officer, how police officers help the community, what skills police officers need, and what tools and equipment police officers use to help them do their job.

THINGS TO CONSIDER

Call your local police department to request that a police officer visit your school or program. Speak directly to the officer who will be visiting your class. Give her some background information to ensure a successful experience.

○ Tell the officer how old the children are.

○ Be clear about how long the visit should be.

○ Tell the officer about *Officer Buckle and Gloria* and about the safety-related explorations the children have done.

○ Ask the officer to bring appropriate props related to safety to show the children.

○ Find out how the officer would like to be addressed by the children.

STEP BY STEP

1. Facilitate the police officer's visit by doing the following:
   ▢ Suggest topics for the officer to talk about, if necessary.
   ▢ Help the officer understand the children's questions and comments, by rewording them as needed.
   ▢ Encourage the children to ask thoughtful questions. *Jacob, you wanted to ask a question about how our visitor learned how to be a police officer. That would be a good question to ask.*
   ▢ Incorporate the children's ideas or experiences. You might say: *Madison, the officer might like to hear about your mother's job because she helps with safety also.*
   ▢ Take some photographs of the visit to extend the experience.

2. Later the same day or the next day, ask the children to recall details of the officer's visit. Make a chart: "Things We Learned from Officer _____." Write the children's names and their memories of the visit. Encourage them to draw, paint, or dramatize what they remember from the officer's visit.

3. Reread the part of *Officer Buckle and Gloria* where the children send Officer Buckle thank-you notes. Help the children do the same for the officer who visited your group.

Talk with Children

○ Build connections between the police officer's visit and *Officer Buckle and Gloria*. Ask: *What's the same? What's different?*

○ Share your observations as the children draw pictures: *I notice that you drew a special hat on the officer's head. Tell me about that hat.*

Observe Children

○ What do different children observe during the police officer's visit? Do they notice her clothing? Special equipment? Police dog? The siren on her police car?

○ How do the children recall the visit after it's over? Do they talk about it? Draw pictures about it? Dramatize it? Tell about it at home?

○ In what ways do the children show a heightened awareness of safety? Make notes of children who quote the visiting officer, refer to *Officer Buckle and Gloria*, or warn friends of dangerous situations.

EXTEND THE LEARNING

Collect books that have police officers in them to expand the children's thinking about the role of police officers in the community.

Interviewing is an important research skill. Invite other kinds of safety personnel to visit your classroom, such as a lifeguard, a factory safety person, a crossing guard, or ski patrol.

Explore how dogs and other animals help people stay safe. Find out more about how police officers, firefighters, water rescuers, and people with special needs use animals in their work or in their lives.

Add police officer clothing and safety props to your dramatic play area.

CONNECT WITH FAMILIES

Display *Officer Buckle and Gloria* and the chart you made after the officer's visit. Post these items along with the information that follows.

How Do You Do, Officer?

We read *Officer Buckle and Gloria* and we wanted to learn more about a real-life police officer, so we invited Officer _____ to visit our class. The police officer told us how she makes sure people in our community are safe. Here are some things we learned about:

◘ How people must follow the rules to stay safe,

◘ What police officers wear and the special equipment they carry, and

◘ What officers do in their jobs.

See page 188 for a reproducible copy of this note to families.

What's Needed

large piece of cardboard, foam core,
   or plywood
cardboard tubes, boxes, cones
craft sticks
chenille sticks
straws
heavy paper
tape, glue, fasteners

Social Studies Standards

People, Places, and Environments

○ Using personal experiences as a basis for exploring geographic concepts and skills

Power, Authority, and Governance

○ Understanding that there can be different rules in different contexts
○ Becoming effective problem solvers and decision makers

EXPLORATION:

SAFETY RULES

Children create a model playground out of paper, cardboard, and recycled materials. They then write safety rules for this playground.

THINGS TO CONSIDER

Spend time with the children on the playground at your program, looking carefully at all the structures; or visit a playground in your community. Provide ample time for children to play and explore a variety of types of playground equipment.

Take pictures of different playgrounds. Use these as models for the playground you create in class.

STEP BY STEP

1. Tell the children that you are going to make a model playground together. If you can't go to a real playground, brainstorm with them the types of equipment they have played on before.
2. Make a list of all the items the children want to put on the playground. Discuss as a group where on the playground each item should go.
3. Invite the children to design and build a playground. Use a large piece of cardboard, foam core, or plywood as a base on which to build the playground. Encourage the children to tape, glue, and fasten recycled materials together to make play structures, such as:

cardboard tube tunnels	craft stick teeter-totters
chenille stick and straw swing sets	paper slides
cardboard box sand boxes	cone climbing domes

4. When the playground is finished, discuss the rules you need to make the playground safe and fun for everyone. Post these rules next to the playground.

Talk with Children

Encourage the children to take risks and solve challenging problems in creating the playground. Be willing to help, but be sure to let them follow through on their own ideas.

Talk about why you might need rules on a playground. Ask:

What could happen on the playground if there are no rules?
How can rules help everyone have a good time?
How can rules help everyone be safe?

SOCIAL STUDIES AND ME!

Observe Children

Watch the children work and notice who is the most effective at problem-solving and decision-making. It may not be the same children who are your usual leaders.

Notice the different ways children solve problems, make decisions, and share them with the group.

EXTEND THE LEARNING

Encourage the children to create really silly rules and follow up their implications. Here are some possibilities:

What would happen if there were a rule that children could only go up the slide?
What would happen if no grown-ups were allowed on this playground?
What would happen if no talking were allowed?

Use this experiment in silliness as a way to help children see how important good rules are.

CONNECT WITH FAMILIES

In the hall or some other place that is visited frequently by the families, make a table display to exhibit the children's playground and the list of playground rules. Set out the book *Officer Buckle and Gloria* and post the following:

Safety Rules

After reading *Officer Buckle and Gloria*, we talked about what we would like on a playground and what rules we would have so everyone could have a good time and be safe. We learned about:

- Becoming effective problem solvers and decision makers,
- Rules for keeping us safe, and
- Being responsible.

See page 188 for a reproducible copy of this note to families.

SOCIAL STUDIES AND ME!

CHAPTER 5

Communities

INTRODUCING THE THEME

SPARKING CURIOSITY

What do you think of when you hear the word community? You might start thinking about different kinds of communities—schools, neighborhoods, towns, and cities. Perhaps the places and buildings of a community come to mind—houses, apartment buildings, stores, churches, roads, parks, playgrounds. Or maybe you think of all the different people that make up a community—teachers, doctors, police officers, firefighters, mayors, shopkeepers, hairdressers. Then again, you might begin thinking about the less tangible qualities of communities—shared experiences, common goals, a sense of security, a feeling of belonging.

Communities are all of these things. They are webs that keep people connected to each other. It takes many people doing many different things to keep communities alive and well. Thinking about communities provides an excellent opportunity for young children to explore and experience important social studies skills, attitudes, and knowledge.

When early childhood educators work to build a strong sense of community within a group of children, the children learn to participate in community life. They learn to:

○ Assert their own rights and respect the rights of others,
○ Take responsibility for the care of common space,
○ Abide by rules and follow routines, and
○ Receive help from and give help to others.

BUILDING BACKGROUND

When children explore beyond their school or child care center on walks or field trips, they meet people, see places, and experience first-hand the interesting sights and sounds of the community. They learn about:

○ The many different jobs that people do,
○ New and old buildings in the community,
○ How technology is used in many different ways, and
○ Different ways to get from one place in the community to another.

Good books encourage children to use their imaginations and sophisticated thinking skills as they read about a variety of communities. They learn to:

○ Use new community-related vocabulary words,
○ Compare book illustrations with real communities,
○ Identify how story characters work together just like real people, and
○ Evaluate the choices characters make and think about their own choices.

Some ideas to start you thinking about social studies:

Idea For young children, learning about communities sets the stage for understanding very sophisticated social studies concepts: the economics of goods and services, the impact of technology on people, and the processes of producing and consuming.

Idea Introduce a song about community workers. As children's vocabulary and knowledge grows, add new workers and information about their jobs. Sing to the tune of "The Farmer in the Dell." For example,

The pilot on the plane,
The pilot on the plane,
This is someone that we know.
The pilot on the plane.

SOCIAL STUDIES AND ME!

Some ideas to start you thinking about language and literacy:

Idea Thinking about communities includes thinking about how we communicate. Children read about communities, engage in community investigations, and experience a sense of community with one another. They will be communicating orally with a variety of individuals both old and young, and they will see the great number of ways written communication is used through print and symbols.

Idea Have fun with poetry! If you want to sing a poem, then sing it. If you only want to use one verse (first, last, or one in the middle) then do that. Find more poems at your library that have a community theme.

Poem:

The Muffin Man

Do you know the muffin man,
The muffin man, the muffin man,
Oh, do you know the muffin man,
Who lives in Drury Lane?

Yes I know the muffin man,
The muffin man, the muffin man,
Oh yes, I know the muffin man,
Who lives in Drury Lane!
　　　　　　　—Traditional

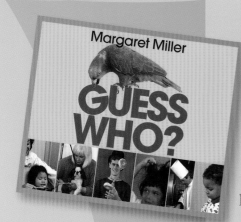

Margaret Miller
GUESS WHO?

Vocabulary

guess: to think or suppose something, to form an opinion without knowing for sure

umpire: someone who enforces the rules of the game in sports

veterinarian: someone qualified in the medical treatment of animals, an animal doctor

Social Studies Standards

Individuals, Groups, and Institutions

○ Understanding family structures, careers, and roles

Civic Ideals and Practices

○ Understanding how an individual can make a positive difference in the community

BOOK TALK

Children think about the people in the community who help us. Children are asked, "Who delivers the mail?" "Who cuts people's hair?" "Who flies an airplane?" and who performs other important tasks. Each question has several different answers from which to choose before the answer is revealed. Large, color photographs are perfect for guessing and discussing.

MAKING CONNECTIONS

What do children know about the work community helpers do? What jobs can they name and describe? What are the names of the places where those workers do their jobs?

Create a word web of the children's responses. Check the responses against the jobs in *Guess Who?*

SOCIAL STUDIES AND ME!

INTRODUCING THE BOOK

Share the cover of the book. Point to the picture of the girl in the dentist's chair. Ask:

What is happening in this picture?
Have you ever been to the dentist? What happened there?

Looking at the chef, you might ask:

What do you think this man is doing?
What do you think a hat like that might be for?

Continue, having the children look carefully at the other pictures on the cover and describe what is happening.

Read the title aloud. Explain that this book is a guessing game about people who work in the community.

READING AND TALKING TOGETHER

○ The book provides lots of opportunities to talk about what kinds of jobs people do, where they work, how they help us, and what experiences the children have had with them in their own lives.

○ Read the book aloud, pausing for the children to share their ideas and to ask and answer the "Guess who?" questions. For example: *Does a crab fix cars? Why not?*

○ Talk about the other pictures on the page. What do the children know about a plumber, a clown, a veterinarian, a mechanic? Have they ever had experiences with any of these? What happened? For example:

Have you ever seen someone repair a car? Who was it?
Is someone in your family a mechanic? What does he or she do?

○ Let the children flip through the book and share their favorite community helpers.

What's Needed

the book, *Guess Who?*

paint and paintbrushes

mural paper

drawing paper

glue or tape

Social Studies Standards

Individuals, Groups, and Institutions

○ Understanding family structures, careers, and roles

People, Places, and Environments

○ Matching objects to geographical locations

○ Mapping

Production, Distribution, and Consumption

○ Identifying and discussing the duties of a variety of community occupations

EXPLORATION:

MURAL OF COMMUNITY HELPERS

In this exploration children create a mural of the neighborhood and put community helpers on it.

THINGS TO CONSIDER

Mural painting works best when it is carefully planned and organized. To simplify cleanup, it is best to do the painting in an area with hard surfaces and easy access to water. This exploration will take place over several days, so we recommend working on the murals away from high-traffic areas.

While this activity focuses on a "workers in the neighborhood" concept, it can be adapted to whatever kind of community you live in. Even in very rural areas, there are workers: telephone company workers, truck drivers, farmers, teachers, and school bus drivers. Remember too, you can explore the jobs of the people in the children's own families.

STEP BY STEP

1. Ask the children to name some of the different workers in *Guess Who?* Look through the book together to jog your memories.

2. Tell the children that these workers live and work in communities like yours. Explain that you will be painting a mural of your community and putting workers in it. Hang the mural paper and explain how the big things need to be painted first, before smaller things, like people.

3. Generate a list of everything they want to put on the mural; this will depend on the features of your community. A walk around the neighborhood will stimulate ideas for this list: streets, telephone poles, signs, cars, fences, buildings, trees, and so on. Consider drawing pictures next to the words so pre-readers can use the list independently.

4. As you look at the list with the children, decide which are the big things to paint first. Have the children paint roads, buildings, and trees before smaller details such as signs, birds, and vehicles. Younger children can paint inside teacher-drawn outlines and older children can paint more independently. Everyone can add details as they desire.

5. Refer back to the list of workers, and invite the children to draw or paint community helpers on smaller paper. These can then be cut out and attached to the mural.

Talk with Children

Make connections between workers to demonstrate the community they work in. The veterinarian pays the mechanic to fix her car so she can drive to work. The letter carrier delivers the dentist's mail. The police officer buys bread that the baker made. The baker takes his dog to the veterinarian.

Encourage the children to include community helpers that are not in the book. If a fire engine, garbage truck, or delivery van goes by, use that moment to add those workers to the list.

Observe Children

O Notice what the children know about the neighborhood and what they are most interested in. Follow their interests while also helping them explore areas they know less about.
O Do the children understand that people do their jobs, get paid for their work, and then spend that money on things they need?
O Watch and make notes about whether the children enjoy art projects that require them to work with others.

EXTEND THE LEARNING

Children can write questions similar to the ones in *Guess Who?* and post them around their mural. Run a piece of yarn from each question to the community helper that answers it on the mural.

If the mural or neighborhood walk revealed that children have a particular interest, you could arrange to interview an expert. Police officers, firefighters, delivery persons, veterinarians, and others offer a wealth of information that young children are interested in.

CONNECT WITH FAMILIES

Use the mural as the focal point of your family display. Display the book *Guess Who?*, lists of neighborhood features and workers, and the following note to parents beside the mural.

Mural of Community Helpers

We've been reading *Guess Who?* and studying workers in our community. We painted a mural of the neighborhood and then put workers in it. We learned that:

- Our community is where we live,
- Workers help their community by doing important jobs,
- Some workers' jobs are to keep us safe or take care of us, and other workers' jobs provide us with things we need, and
- People earn money doing their jobs, and use it to pay for the things their families need.

See page 189 for a reproducible copy of this note to families.

What's Needed

camera, video recorder
tape recorder
clipboards with paper
markers or pencils

Social Studies Standards

Production, Distribution, and Consumption

○ Exploring economic decisions and experiences

Science, Technology, and Society

○ Understanding that people invent tools and machines that help them solve problems or do tasks more quickly or easily

EXPLORATION:

LET'S BE RESEARCHERS!

Children visit a community business similar to one featured in *Guess Who?* Children will become active explorers, doing first-hand research to answer the questions they have about different community businesses.

THINGS TO CONSIDER

When you plan a field trip, you need to think about safety and logistics. For this research experience you should also be thinking about how to make it the most effective learning experience. Consider the following:

Will children have opportunities to ask questions?

Will they be able to do something as well as see something?

Will they be able to collect information independently, by questions, observation, or hands-on exploration?

Choose a community business or non-profit organization willing to host a preschool field trip. Gather necessary research tools (such as cameras, video recorders, clipboards with paper, markers or pencils) and pre-selected interview questions.

STEP BY STEP

1. Reread *Guess Who?* to your group. Pay attention to which careers or workplaces fascinate the children the most. Ask questions about a particular career or business that might interest them. For example:

   What do you know about pilots?

   What questions do you have about pilots?

   How could we learn about pilots?

2. Ask these questions about the different businesses or careers that the children show the most interest in. Make notes for yourself about the extent of the children's background knowledge and their questions.

Keep in mind that the more they already know about a topic, the more sophisticated their questions and observations about it will be.

3. Schedule a visit to an appropriate location, planning it far enough in advance so that you can recruit family members to assist you.

4. Brainstorm a list of questions the class will want to ask. During the visit, encourage the children to gather information about the worker by asking questions and observing. Help them record information by drawing and writing, taking photographs or videos, and using the tape recorder.

5. What happens after a field experience is just as important as what happens before and during the outing. Debrief by asking focused but open-ended questions such as:

   What did you notice about the place we visited?
   I noticed you looking carefully at _____ .
   What were you looking for?
   What did you see or hear about what _____ do?
   What other questions do you have?

6. Help the children write and illustrate a class thank-you note to the people at the location you visited.

Talk with Children

Continue to bring children's attention to details of the field trip. Ask:

How could you find out about that?
What do you notice?
Did anything surprise you? What? Why?

Observe Children

○ While you are on the field trip, listen for the language of discovery:

   I have never seen that . . .
   I never knew . . .
   So that's why . . .

○ Notice what the children are interested in, take pictures of it, encourage them to draw or write about it, and ask questions about it.

○ Are the children connecting with a particular "expert"? Make a record of their conversation or photograph their interaction.

EXTEND THE LEARNING

Some teachers like to gather photos from a field trip and put them into a book. If you decide to do this, try to capture every step of the trip, from getting into cars or the bus to arriving back at school. Label the pictures. Encourage the children to look at the pictures and labels and to tell a story about what happened on the field trip.

Invite the children to share other experiences they have had visiting a business near their home. Ask:

What do they do or make there?

Who works there? What did you see them doing?

Do you or your family use what they make?

CONNECT WITH FAMILIES

A three-panel poster board is an excellent way to share with families the photos, drawings, and anecdotes from a field trip. You have room to include the social studies standards covered and the social studies research skills used; plus it lets you publicly thank the family members who helped out. Add a note that says:

Let's Be Researchers!

After we read *Guess Who?* we took a field trip to find out about *[name of business]*. *[Names of family members who helped]* helped make this a very smooth and interesting learning experience.

- We wanted to know what the business [makes/does], who does the work, why they do it and how they do it. As researchers, we
- Explored some jobs done by workers in our community,
- Asked questions, and
- Learned that people use tools and machines to make their jobs easier.

See page 189 for a reproducible copy of this note to families.

SOCIAL STUDIES AND ME!

Book Talk

When Ruby takes Max along to shop for Grandma's birthday present, she has to spend her carefully saved money on things she never anticipated.

MAKING CONNECTIONS

Building an understanding of simple economics with children.

Talk with the children about shopping. Ask:

Who takes you shopping? Where do you go?

What kinds of things do you shop for?

What kinds of things do you get to choose?

Show examples of money, both coins and dollar bills. Ask:

What kinds of money do you know about?

Do you know the names of some of the coins?

What do we use money for?

INTRODUCING THE BOOK

Before you read *Bunny Money*, look at the cover together. Ask:

Do you recognize the character on the cover? What's his name?

Have you read other books about Max?

Can you tell me what his sister's name is?

Look at the "bunny money" in the front and back of the book. Ask:

Is the money all the same? How is it different?

Do you think the money is real? Why or why not?

Flip through the book, looking at the pictures. Invite the children to predict what Max and Ruby will do with the "bunny money." Read the book aloud to find out what happens.

READING AND TALKING TOGETHER

- Be sure to read the whole book in one sitting. This will help the children understand the story.
- After reading the book, talk with the children about the characters: Max, Ruby, and Grandma. Ask:

Who is your favorite character? Why?

How does Ruby feel about Max? How can you tell?

What do Ruby and Max really need to shop for?

What's special about Grandma?

Vocabulary

dollar: unit of money worth 100 cents

penny: coin worth one cent

quarter: coin worth 25 cents

wallet: a small case that holds money and credit cards, usually carried in a pocket or purse

Social Studies Standards

Production, Distribution, and Consumption

- Understanding the difference between wants and needs and making decisions based on this understanding
- Exploring economic decisions and experiences
- Observing, discussing, and dramatizing basic economic concepts such as buying and selling, producing, and consuming
- Understanding money and how it is used

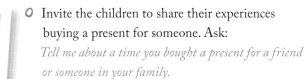

○ Invite the children to share their experiences buying a present for someone. Ask:
Tell me about a time you bought a present for a friend or someone in your family.
How did you choose what to buy?
How did you pay for it?

○ Another time you read the book, use play money and a wallet as props. Each time a dollar (or more) is spent, remove a dollar from the wallet and count how many are left. Be sure to explain to the children that the five-dollar bill represents five one-dollar bills. Demonstrate this with five bills.

EXPLORATION:

WE PRODUCE AND WE BUY

Children make something to sell, set up a store, and then sell their product.

What's Needed

the book, *Bunny Money*

chart paper

your choice of "bunny money" or
  real money

supplies needed for making your
  product

large drawing paper

markers

paint and paintbrushes

Social Studies Standards

Production, Distribution, and Consumption

O Exploring economic decisions and experiences

O Observing, discussing, and dramatizing basic economic concepts such as buying and selling, producing and consuming

O Understanding money and how it is used

O Identifying and discussing the duties of a variety of occupations

THINGS TO CONSIDER

This exploration will take place over time. There are several phases: deciding what to sell, producing the product, setting up the store, and then selling the product.

STEP BY STEP

Decide what to sell

1. Invite the children to think about what they might like to make and sell in a classroom store.

2. Use your knowledge of the group and what is currently going on in the classroom to guide the choice. You might grow vegetable and flower seedlings, make cookies, or do a craft project children really enjoy.

Make the product

1. Tell the children you are going to set up a factory to make (grow, build) your product. Separate the project into specific jobs. For example, in a seedling nursery, some children will be putting soil in pots, some will be planting seeds, and some will be watering the planted pots and putting them in the window.

2. Make sure every child has a job. Then let them get started!

Set up the store

1. Brainstorm items a store needs. Look back at *Bunny Money* for ideas. (Rosalinda's Gift Shop and Candi's Corner have product displays, signs, and a cash register.) Help the children collect the items or make them from classroom materials and props.

2. Fill the shelves with your product. Decide how much the product will cost. It should be a simple amount like $1.00 or $2.00 so that the cashier's job will be easier.

3. Determine when the store will be open for business. Advertise in your family newsletter or hang signs in the school or neighborhood to attract customers.

4. Assign jobs for the store, such as cashiers, stockers, floor clerks, and greeters. Then open for business! If you have decided to use "bunny money" instead of real money, the greeters can give customers the bills at the door.

Talk with Children

As the children are designing the store, ask:

What stores have you been in?

What is the same about all stores? What is different?

How do workers in stores talk to customers?

Observe Children

O What do the children know about factories and stores?

O Are they using language such as close, open, work, price, buy, and sell?

O How are they acting like workers?

O Has the "factory" and "setting up shop" work carried over into their play?

EXTEND THE LEARNING

If you ran the store with real money, decide with the children what the money will be used for. Perhaps you could donate it to a charity children think is important, or use it to buy special art supplies or books for the classroom.

Make class books called "Our Factory" and "Our Store," documenting the exploration in the children's own words.

Provide more information about producing and selling products by providing additional books, field trips, or expert visitors.

CONNECT WITH FAMILIES

In a place that is accessible and visible to families, set up a display. Include *Bunny Money*, a product sample, signs or other artifacts, and photos of the exploration. Post the following to inform families of the learning that took place.

We Produce and We Buy

We had so much fun reading *Bunny Money* that we decided to make our own store. First, we had to make [name of your product] in our factory, and then we set up a shop. Customers came and bought our product.

We learned that:

- People work in factories,
- Factories produce things for stores to sell,
- People work in stores, and
- Stores sell things to people who want or need them.

See page 190 for a reproducible copy of this note to families.

EXPLORATION:

THE FURTHER ADVENTURES OF MAX

In this exploration, children write a new story about how Max and Ruby might spend their money.

What's Needed
the book, *Bunny Money*
chart paper
drawing paper
crayons
markers
colored pencils

Social Studies Standards
Production, Distribution, and Consumption
O Understanding the difference between wants and needs and making decisions based on this understanding
O Exploring economic decisions and experiences
O Understanding money and how it is used

THINGS TO CONSIDER

What do children already know about needs and wants? Clarify misconceptions about needs and wants by helping children see that many of the things that people would like to have (or already have) are wants rather than needs.

Tap into children's prior knowledge about spending and saving money. Guide further discussions based on their level of understanding of these concepts.

STEP BY STEP

1. Reread *Bunny Money* to make sure children know the characters Max, Ruby, and Grandma. Review the story's plot: Max and Ruby have a problem. What can they buy Grandma for her birthday? They have many adventures before they solve the problem.

2. Think about new adventures Max and Ruby might have with the money. Here are some ideas to get you thinking.
   Max and Ruby lose the wallet with the money and they . . .
   Max and Ruby decide to go on a trip with their money and they . . .
   Max and Ruby decide to save the money so they . . .
   Have the group decide on a basic idea for a new story.

3. Remind the children that most stories involve a problem that needs to be solved. Ask:
   What is the problem that needs to be solved in our story?
   How can Max and Ruby solve it?

4. Invite the children to add details and events. Take notes on chart paper. Stop from time to time to summarize the story so far. Then ask: *What happens next?*

5. Read the finished story aloud. Let individual children select which parts of the story they want to illustrate. Put their drawings together, add captions from your notes, and put the story together into a big book.

Talk with Children

Children may need help keeping the story on track. Ask leading questions and make comments about the story as you go along. For example:
Now the story has a problem! What are some solutions to Max and Ruby's problem? What happens next?
How might Max and Ruby decide to spend the money? What's the difference between what Max wants and what Ruby wants?

Observe Children

O Do the children repeat events that they have heard in other stories or do they create new plot twists for this story?

O Do the children refer back to *Bunny Money* as they add to their new story?

O Make notes of children who are hesitant to participate in the activity. How can the activity be adapted to involve them?

EXTEND THE LEARNING

Follow up this activity with additional language-based explorations such as these.

O Write a letter to Ruby to suggest ways she can help Max spend his money more wisely.

O Brainstorm what Max might do if he had more money.

O Create and perform a chant or song about *Bunny Money*.

O Act out the new story written by the class.

CONNECT WITH FAMILIES

Display *Bunny Money* and "The Further Adventures of Max and Ruby" big book where families can enjoy them. Post the following on your bulletin board:

The Further Adventures of Max and Ruby

After we read *Bunny Money* we decided to write another adventure starring Max and Ruby. We learned that most stories have a problem to be solved. Max and Ruby have a BIG problem in our story! As we followed our favorite bunny characters, we also learned about:

◘ The difference between needs and wants,

◘ Saving and spending money, and

◘ Making choices about money.

See page 190 for a reproducible copy of this note to families.

SOCIAL STUDIES AND ME!

Book Talk

In this "Who am I?" story, a garbage truck tells us about the stinky work he and his crew do at night. Children will love the alphabet of garbage at the center of this book!

MAKING CONNECTIONS

A garbage truck is one kind of truck that is used to do a job. Talk with the children about other trucks. Ask:

What kinds of trucks can you name?

Do you know anyone who uses a truck for work?

What work does she do?

INTRODUCING THE BOOK

Share the cover with the children. Pinch your nose as you read the title. Children love words like stink. Ask:

What kind of truck do you think this is?

Why do you think the authors named this book "I Stink!?"

Look at the picture on the back cover. Ask:

What does it look like the truck is doing?

How do we know, when we look at pictures, whether someone is awake or asleep?

Look at and talk about the endpapers (the pages at the back of the book). Talk about what the children see in the squares.

READING AND TALKING TOGETHER

O Before reading the book to the children, practice reading it several times. You'll need to become a talking garbage truck with lots of expression!

O Read the book aloud, pausing to look at the art and ask questions.

What does the truck do at night?

What is in the truck's alphabet soup?

What is your favorite part of the story?

O Talk about garbage.

How do different families in our class get rid of their garbage?

What would happen if we just let garbage pile up?

How do you think people in the past got rid of garbage?

Brainstorm ways people in the future might dispose of garbage.

Vocabulary

biodegradable: made of substances that will decay relatively quickly as a result of the action of bacteria

brakes: the part of a machine that slows it down or stops it

dual op: having two of every control system

hopper: a large funnel-shaped receptacle for fuel or other materials

steering wheel: the wheel in a vehicle that is turned to change the direction of travel

throttle: a valve used to control the amount of fuel and air entering the cylinders of an engine

Social Studies Standards

People, Places, and Environments

O Talking about and dramatizing transportation and movement, including how animals move

Production, Distribution, and Consumption

O Identifying and discussing the duties of a variety of occupations

What's Needed

the book, *I Stink!*

collection of clean garbage or
     pictures of garbage

recycle bin

chart paper

markers

Social Studies Standards

Civic Ideals and Practices

○ Understanding how an
   individual can make a positive
   difference in the community

**Production, Distribution, and
Consumption**

○ Identifying and discussing the
   duties of a variety of
   occupations

**Power, Authority, and
Governance**

○ Becoming effective problem
   solvers and decision makers

Time, Continuity, and Change

○ Understanding how the world
   has changed and how it might
   change in the future

EXPLORATION:

GARBAGE MONSTER

Children chart what gets thrown out in the classroom and learn about ways of reducing, reusing, and recycling.

THINGS TO CONSIDER

Children will come to this exploration with widely varied experiences with recycling. Be sure to present recycling in an upbeat, "we can all help" way, rather than a scary "save the dying planet" way.

For cleanliness and safety reasons, create your own selection of garbage rather than have the children go into the actual garbage can. You'll need a balance of paper, plastic, food scraps, and so on. Pictures also work well.

In advance, you may want to check what materials your local recycling center takes.

STEP BY STEP

1. Show the children the page in *I Stink!* that lists all the kinds of garbage the truck picked up. Together, discuss where the garbage goes. Introduce the concepts of reduce, reuse, and recycle.

2. Have the children sit in a circle. Dump the garbage in the center of the circle. Talk about what each item is made of. Point out the recycle symbol on items that have them.

3. The children can sort the garbage, placing recyclable materials in a bin.

4. Make a T-chart to show which things can be recycled or reused and which must be thrown out. Refer to and add to the chart over time. For example, after snack or an art activity children can look at the table and decide which things could be recycled.

SOCIAL STUDIES AND ME!

Talk with Children

Encourage the children to talk about ways to reuse things. Ask:
Why would we want to make less garbage?

Children love to use big words! Introduce the word biodegradable and encourage them to use it. Some children may want to talk about how their families recycle and deal with garbage.

Observe Children

Observe children as they work.

○ Do they understand that garbage is made of different materials? (Magazines and newspapers are paper, milk jugs and yogurt containers are plastic, soup cans are metal.)

○ Are the children listening to each other's ideas?

○ What kinds of information do the children offer about protecting the environment?

EXTEND THE LEARNING

Have the children fill a container with soil and bury several different kinds of garbage. Keep it damp. It can be dug up multiple times over the next months to see what has (or hasn't) changed.

Visit a local recycling center with the children; interview the workers about what can be recycled. Set up a system for recycling in the classroom if you do not have one already.

Children will have fun drawing and writing about new items to add to the garbage truck's alphabet soup.

CONNECT WITH FAMILIES

Display *I Stink!* near the bulletin board with the "What Can Be Recycled? What Can Be Reused?" chart. Record children's comments from the discussion of the book and exploration; display them as well. Post the following:

Collecting Garbage

Reading *I Stink!* got us thinking about garbage. Where does all the garbage go? We talked about our classroom garbage and made a chart showing what we could recycle or reuse.

As we sorted and talked, we thought about:

▢ Our impact on the environment,

▢ How our actions can help keep our world clean, and

▢ Ways to reuse materials to cut down on waste.

See page 191 for a reproducible copy of this note to families.

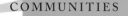

What's Needed

the book, *I Stink!*

books about or pictures of vehicles

empty appliance boxes

smaller empty boxes

large plastic lids

paper towel tubes

chart paper

markers

glue, masking tape

paint and paintbrushes

Social Studies Standards

People, Places, and Environments

○ Talking about and dramatizing transportation and movement, including how animals move

Science, Technology, and Society

○ Understanding that people invent tools and machines that help them solve problems or do tasks more quickly or easily

EXPLORATION:

BUILD A VEHICLE

In this exploration children learn about different modes of transportation and use creativity to build their own vehicles.

THINGS TO CONSIDER

Decide if the children will work together to build one vehicle or if they will work in smaller groups and build several vehicles. Children will use a lot of found materials when they build, so be sure to collect plenty of boxes and other supplies for this investigation. This project may take many days to complete so plan accordingly.

An adult will have to cut doors in the appliance boxes so that the children can climb into their vehicles.

A few notes about collecting the boxes for this project:

Call a local appliance retailer to get their cast-off boxes.

You will need lots of smaller boxes in a variety of sizes and shapes.

A note home to families requesting specific materials often yields great results.

STEP BY STEP

1. Tell the children you are going to build vehicles. Remind them that *I Stink!* is about one kind of vehicle with a specific job. Make a chart of other kinds of vehicles the children know about and what each is used for.

2. Help the children decide what kind of vehicle they want to build, and then brainstorm what parts that vehicle needs. For example, fire engines need wheels, hoses, and ladders.)

3. Set out the appliance boxes and invite the children to use them as the base for their vehicle. Children can select any of the other materials to create details and special features for their vehicle. They may want to consult books or pictures to decide what details to add.

4. Allow plenty of time for the children to work on their vehicles. When the vehicles are done, they will want to play with them for several days.

SOCIAL STUDIES AND ME!

Talk with Children

Encourage children to think about how people use their work vehicles, such as putting out fires, plowing snow, digging holes, or transporting materials or people. Ask: *What extra things does your vehicle need to do its job?*

When the vehicles are finished, encourage the children to use them for dramatic play. Say:

Look, those workers need to dig a cellar hole.
The fire alarm is ringing; let's go put out the fire!
The grocery store is out of milk. Let's load the truck and deliver some.

Observe Children

- Notice how different children build. Do they have a plan or do they work spontaneously? Do they consult pictures for details or work from memory?
- Listen for children who know the names of vehicles and the parts of vehicles.
- Are the children able to listen to each other's ideas and build cooperatively?
- Are they making connections between the parts of the vehicle and their functions?

EXTEND THE LEARNING

Go on a "vehicle hunt" around the neighborhood. What kind of vehicles do the children see? What do people use them for?

Animals move from one place to another in many different ways. Gather pictures of different animals. Talk about the different ways animals move. Which fly? Which swim? Do some of them slither? Do some of them crawl? Have the children sort the animals by their movements.

Sign songs about familiar vehicles, such as "The Wheels on the Bus," "A Peanut Sat on a Railroad Track," or "Down by the Station."

CONNECT WITH FAMILIES

The finished cardboard box vehicles will be the gathering place for families as children clamor to share their finished work. Take advantage of the excitement by displaying other materials from the exploration, including the book *I Stink!* and this message:

Build a Vehicle

Reading *I Stink!* made us curious about different kinds of vehicles and what people use them for. We built vehicles in the classroom. As we did this we talked about:

- How we have vehicles for different purposes, and
- The kinds of specialized tools and vehicles workers use to do their jobs.

See page 191 for a reproducible copy of this note to families.

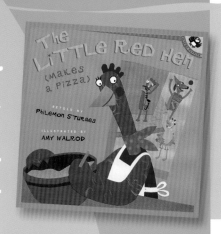

Vocabulary

delicatessen: a store that sells ready-to-serve foods such as cheeses, cold cooked meats, and salads

fetch: to go after and bring back somebody or something

knead: to fold, press and stretch a soft substance such as dough, working it into a smooth mass

rummage: to look quickly for something by carelessly moving and disarranging things

Social Studies Standards

Power, Authority, and Governance
O Exploring the concept of fairness in our relationships with others

Time, Continuity, and Change
O Understanding the links between human decisions and their consequences

Production, Distribution, and Consumption
O Observing, discussing, and dramatizing basic economic concepts such as buying and selling, producing and consuming

Book Talk

In this contemporary re-telling of *The Little Red Hen*, the hen decides to make a pizza. When the hen's friends refuse to help, she makes the pizza herself. This version of the story offers a twist where the friends find a way to help out after all!

Making Connections

Engage children in a conversation about helping each other. Talk together about:
O Ways in which children are helpers in their families,
O Ways people in their families help the children, and
O Ways children are helpers in their classroom.

Ask questions about community helpers.
Do you know anyone in our community who is a helper?
What does he or she do?
Whom does this person help?

Introducing the Book

Look at the front and back covers for clues about the story. The children may remember another story about the Little Red Hen. Invite volunteers to tell that story in their own words. Explain that in this new story, the hen makes pizza.

Study and talk about the title page. Point to and have the children name the ingredients. Ask: *What do you like on your pizza?*

Reading and Talking Together

O Read the story, letting the children enjoy the humor in this zany tale.
O Read the story again. Then do a picture walk, looking carefully and talking about each picture. There are funny things on almost every page. Ask:
What items and ingredients can you name?
What are the Dog, the Duck, and the Cat doing on each page?
Why are they dressed the way they are? (You may have to explain about the "jazzy, cool cat.")
How do you think the artist made the illustrations?

O This is a great book for responsive reading. By the time you get to the third round of "Not I" the children will chime in (with your encouragement) and repeat, "Very well then, I'll fetch it myself."

SOCIAL STUDIES AND ME!

EXPLORATION:

ACT IT OUT

Children will act out the story *The Little Red Hen (Makes a Pizza)*, deciding on props, costumes, and how the story should be told.

What's Needed
the book, *The Little Red Hen (Makes a Pizza)*
props (bowl, pan, spoon)
costumes

Social Studies Standards
Civic Ideals and Practices
O Understanding the balance between rights and responsibilities

Production, Distribution, and Consumption
O Understanding the difference between wants and needs and making decisions based on this understanding
O Exploring economic decisions and experiences

THINGS TO CONSIDER

Some children will need lots of guidance to act out the story. Other children will want to direct the whole project. Assign roles and responsibilities to take advantage of each child's strengths and interests.

Organizing and directing a classroom play can be challenging. You might be the narrator/director and the children can be actors and stagehands.

STEP BY STEP

1. With your group, look through *The Little Red Hen (Makes a Pizza)* and decide which props you already have in your classroom and which props and costumes the children would like to make. The book can be divided into five scenes:
   hardware store scene
   supermarket scene
   delicatessen scene
   "making the pizza" scene
   eating and cleaning up scene

2. For each scene, decide who will play the role of the Little Red Hen, Dog, Cat, and Duck.

3. Encourage the actors to really show expressions by giving direction such as:
   Little Red Hen, show how frustrated you are that nobody is helping!
   Duck, Dog, and Cat, look lazy and yawn when the hen asks you to help!

4. If possible, take photographs of the young actors and actresses.

5. Consider performing the play for families.

Talk with Children

Invite all the children to chime in when the Little Red Hen asks for help. This will give them practice for when they play the roles of Dog, Duck, or Cat. Ask:
What do Cat, Dog and Duck say now?

When children ask for help in the classroom, remind them about the Little Red Hen. Say: *I see you need help just like the Little Red Hen did. I'll be glad to help you.*

Observe Children

o Which children want to be the "stars" of the role play? Which stay in the background? Does repeating the play several times help some children get over their initial reluctance?

o If possible, use the camera as an observation tool. Share pictures of the play with the children to help them remember what it was like to play their roles.

o A video recorder is another tool you may want to try. Ask a family member to record the play and then show it to your group.

EXTEND THE LEARNING

Retell the Little Red Hen story with a different ending in which everyone cooperates. Everyone goes to the store, helps with the shopping, makes the pizza, and helps to clean up.

Ask the children to help you retell the new version of the story. You might say something like: *What would happen if the Duck, the Cat, and the Dog were really helpful and cooperative?*

Take notes as the group retells the story. Stop often and summarize what the children have said. Remind the children that the animals are now helping each other.

Retell the new story and allow the children to act it out.

CONNECT WITH FAMILIES

Hold a performance of the play and invite families to attend. After the performance, share with families *The Little Red Hen (Makes a Pizza)* storybook, photographs you have taken of the children as they acted out the story, and the following information on a poster.

Role Play

We read *The Little Red Hen (Makes a Pizza)* and then we acted out the story. In the story, nobody cooperates with the Little Red Hen in making the pizza, but they are all ready to help eat it!

Here are some social studies ideas we are learning about:

▫ Understanding the difference between things we want and things we need,

▫ Making decisions based on money and resources,

▫ Understanding the balance between rights and responsibilities, and

▫ Understanding how an individual can make a positive difference in the community.

See page 192 for a reproducible copy of this note to families.

SOCIAL STUDIES AND ME!

EXPLORATION:

CREATE A RESTAURANT

Children explore different jobs in a restaurant and the people who do them.

What's Needed
chart paper

markers

classroom furniture

props (silverware, dishes, pretend food, pots and pans)

Social Studies Standards
Production, Distribution, and Consumption

○ Observing, discussing, and dramatizing basic economic concepts such as buying and selling, producing, and consuming

○ Understanding money and how it is used

○ Identifying and discussing the duties of a variety of occupations

THINGS TO CONSIDER

This exploration can take place over many days, even weeks. Schedule some time each day for the children to work on the project.

Children will have a wide variety of restaurant experiences, from ordering at the counter of a fast food restaurant to being waited on by servers, and everything in between. Be sure to value all their information, because: *There are different types of restaurants.*

How the classroom restaurant looks will depend on the children's ideas and experience, so listen carefully.

STEP BY STEP

1. Tell the children that the Little Red Hen making pizza to feed her friends and family reminds you of a restaurant. Explain that your group will create its own restaurant. Ask: *What do you know about restaurants?*

2. Plan the restaurant together. Ask the children:
   What kind of a restaurant should we make?
   What will we need to make a restaurant?
   Write down all of their ideas.

3. Using the children's ideas, work together to set up a restaurant. You can gather play food, pictures of food, or even real food. The children may want to make menus, placemats, signs, order slips, and money for the restaurant.

4. Talk about the different jobs in a restaurant, and let the children choose their roles: customer, waiter/waitress, cashier, host/hostess, cook, and dishwasher.

5. Play "Restaurant"!

Talk with Children

Listen carefully to the children's ideas. Ask questions to help them explore their own thinking.
Who seats the customers?
How does the customer know what kinds of food the restaurant serves?
How does the cook know what to make?
How does everyone know how much the food costs?

Observe Children

Listen to children as they play.

○ Do they understand how all the workers cooperate to run the restaurant?

○ Do they understand that customers pay money for food and service?

○ Do you need to provide them with more information about restaurants through books, interviewing "experts," or field trips?

EXTEND THE LEARNING

A class trip to a local restaurant will enrich the children's understanding. Ask them:
What do you want to know about restaurants?

Write down all of their questions and bring the list with you. When you return from the trip, add the information you gathered to a "what we learned about restaurants" list.

Sing songs and chants about restaurant foods, such as "On Top of Spaghetti," "Patty Cake," "Peanut Butter and Jelly," and "Mix a Pancake."

Make individual pizzas. Post a recipe for making pizzas on English muffin halves. Set out the toppings and let the children prepare their own treats. Heat and eat! (Note: be sure to check for food allergies before doing this activity.)

CONNECT WITH FAMILIES

Display *The Little Red Hen (Makes a Pizza)*, charts, samples of menus, money, and other restaurant props. If possible, include photos of the classroom restaurant in action with the following:

Create a Restaurant

After reading *The Little Red Hen (Makes a Pizza)* we began thinking about restaurants and the people who work in them. We decided to set up a restaurant in our classroom. We talked about:

▢ The different jobs people who work in restaurants do,

▢ How all of the restaurant workers cooperate in order to be successful,

▢ How a restaurant needs customers so it can earn money to pay the workers, and

▢ How customers pay money for the food they eat and the service they receive.

See page 192 for a reproducible copy of this note to families.

SOCIAL STUDIES AND ME!

My Map Book
by Sara Fanelli

To Be a Kid
by Maya Ajmera and
John D. Ivanko

*Where Are You Going
Manyoni?*
by Catherine Stock

CHAPTER 6

The Big World

INTRODUCING THE THEME

SPARKING CURIOSITY

Even for adults, it is difficult to comprehend the size of the earth and the number
of people who live on this planet, let alone the complexities of diverse cultures,
languages, and politics.

There is a lot about the world that young children will not be able fully to
understand, but there are some key ideas and skills they can begin to develop.
Consider the following ways in which young children can be social studies
explorers.

O They can ask questions about people and the earth:
   Do some people live where there is no snow?
   How big is the ocean?

○ They can collect information about the world:

Cities are crowded.

My uncle flew in an airplane to come visit me.

We don't have many houses on our road.

○ They can make geographic and cultural comparisons:

That place is dry and this place is wet.

She walks to school and I take a bus.

He speaks Spanish and I speak English.

I eat with chopsticks and you use a fork.

○ They can arrive at some conclusions about the world:

The world is as big as a giant.

I drew a circle—it's the world.

Everybody in the world goes to school.

BUILDING BACKGROUND

As adults, we often take what we know about people and places in the world for granted; but when we break that body of knowledge into smaller pieces, we begin to realize just how much children need to learn. Even young children can begin learning that:

○ People around the world do many of the same things but in different ways,

○ Maps can be made and used for many different purposes,

○ Sometimes it takes more time to go a longer distance,

○ Maps and globes are special kinds of pictures of the land and water,

○ People around the world have different ways of eating and sleeping, and

○ People and animals can and do move from one place to another.

SOCIAL STUDIES AND ME!

Some ideas to start you thinking about social studies:

Idea
Understanding people, places and environments is important to social studies, and maps are an important aspect of this learning. Preschool children are beginning to enjoy looking at simple, pictorial maps, while globes, atlases, and road maps have little meaning for them. Simple maps of home, classroom, or playground are a good introduction to mapping because they represent familiar places.

Collect and display samples of simple maps and books about maps. Keep an easel in the art area and encourage attempts at painting maps.

Some ideas to start you thinking about language and literacy:

Idea
Before children can understand mapping, they need a lot of practice hearing and using directional language—words like up, down, on top, beside, behind, next to, over, under, and in front of. Even though most young children do not make a clear distinction between left and right, hearing these words in use will lay the foundation for understanding them later on.

Some poems tell a story, some poems are about feelings, and some poems are just fun, like this well-known riddle. Try to share a poem with your group every day. Point out references to people and places in the poems you share.

As I Was Going to St. Ives
As I was going to St. Ives
I met a man with seven wives.
Each wife had seven sacks.
Each sack had seven cats.
Each cat has seven kits.
Kits, cats, sacks, wives,
How many were going to St. Ives?
                    —Traditional

Book Talk

This thought-provoking book shows us that maps can be about more than countries and highways. We all know about road maps, maps of the world, and charts of the stars. But a map of your family? A map of colors? This book makes us think about what maps can tell us, not only about where to go and how to get there, but also about the relationships between one thing and another.

Vocabulary

map: a diagram of something, such as a route or an area, usually designed to show the location of a place or how to get there

Social Studies Standards

People, Places, and Environments

○ Using personal experiences as a basis for exploring geographic concepts and skills

○ Mapping (neighborhood, classroom, etc.)

○ Using spatial and location words

○ Exploring similarities and differences between their own environment and other places

MAKING CONNECTIONS

Find out what kinds of maps the children are familiar with. Ask: *What is a map? Have you ever seen a map? What did the map show? How would you use a map?*

Talk about how a map is a tool that can help us find a place or give us information about a place.

INTRODUCING THE BOOK

My Map Book is not a book to read from beginning to end, as you would a storybook. Each two-page spread is a visual representation (map) of the author's day, heart, stomach, and so on.

You will want to use the book for talking about and making maps with the children. Children will have fun studying and "reading" the maps themselves.

Share the cover with the children. Read the title and discuss the details in the art.

READING AND TALKING TOGETHER

○ Remind the children that you've already explored a part of this book when you did the "Me and My Family Map" exploration.

○ The explorations for this book are "Map Your Classroom" and "Map Your Neighborhood." You will want to study and talk about the "Map of My Bedroom" and "Map of My Neighborhood" in *My Map Book*.

○ Show the children the "Map of My Bedroom" in the book. Look closely at the details. Ask: *What is in her room?*
As the children supply details, respond to them using location words,
Yes, here is the carpet. It is between the desks and the sister's bed.
She did put slippers on the map, next to her bed.

○ Be sure to talk about all the details in the "Map of My Neighborhood: the buildings, river, cars, and other things the author saw in her neighborhood and included on the map. You will want to point out some of the details for the children, such as her friend Daniel, and Bubu the dog.

○ On another day you might want to make a "Map of My Heart" after studying that spread, and so on.

SOCIAL STUDIES AND ME!

EXPLORATION:

CLASSROOM MAP

Children will work together to make a map of the classroom.

What's Needed

the book, *My Map Book*

chart paper

markers

toy people and animal figures

maps of area restaurants,
    landmarks, attractions

maps of subway, train, or bus routes

Social Studies Standards

People, Places, and
Environments

O Using personal experiences as a
   basis for exploring geographic
   concepts and skills

O Matching objects to
   geographical locations

O Mapping

O Using spatial and location
   words

THINGS TO CONSIDER

You will want to do this exploration in several parts, saving the actual mapmaking for a second session, and then using the map in the third session.

Clear some floor space near a wall so all the children can sit against the wall and look at the classroom from the same perspective. In the weeks leading up to this exploration, have maps available in the classroom.

Like the maps in *My Map Book*, this classroom map will not be a perfect, to scale map. While you will be the one drawing the map, think of it as recording the children's ideas, not your own. The things that are most important to the children should be bigger on the map. Mapping is abstract and complicated, which is why the pictures in *My Map Book* are so effective for young children. Keep your map like the ones in the book: simple, colorful, and child-centered.

STEP BY STEP

1. Tell the children they are going to make a map of the classroom. Ask what they want to show on the classroom map. List all of the children's suggestions on chart paper. Include the big areas of the room as well as the small details children want to focus on.

2. Tell the children they are going to sit where they can all see the room the same way. Have them move to the spot you picked and sit down, preferably with their backs against a wall, and all facing in the same direction.

3. Post chart paper in front of the group and draw, as big as you can, an outline of the room. It is important that the children are looking at the map the same way they are looking at the room. Therefore, the wall you draw on the bottom of the map is the wall they are leaning against. Have the children point to each wall in turn, as you draw each wall on the map.

4. Choose one item from the children's list that takes up a lot of space near a wall, such as the block area or the book corner. Tell them, *The book corner belongs on our map; it goes right here.* Be inspired by *My Map Book* and draw simply, in a way children can relate to, perhaps just a bunch of books, or a smiling child reading near a shelf.

5. Once the first "landmark" is on the map, turn to the children for help. Pick another big item from the list and ask the children where it goes on the map. Draw and label it. Keep adding to the map, big things first and then smaller details, asking the children where to place each item as you go.

6. When the map is done ask the children to follow a simple route. They can use a person or animal figure to "walk" on the map to show how to get from one place to another. For example:

   Crystal just put away the playdough and now she wants to read a book. How will she get to the book shelf? Could she get there a different way?

Talk with Children

Use positional/directional vocabulary.

Yes, the dress-up area is next to the blocks.
The art shelf is near the round table.
She walks around the sensory table to the cubbies.
The circle rug is in the middle of the room.

SOCIAL STUDIES AND ME!

Observe Children

O Do the children understand basic positional concepts such as in front of, next to, behind?

O Which children use this vocabulary in their conversations?

O Which children are comfortable with mapping and which are not?

EXTEND THE LEARNING

Encourage the children to make their own classroom maps. Interested children may also want to map their bedrooms, backyards, playgrounds, or other familiar places.

Help the children build a very simple obstacle course using blocks, furniture, large cardboard boxes, and other classroom materials. Make sure that it is designed so you can use words such as: over, under, through, around, behind, beside, between, above, and below to describe location and position. Let the children test the obstacle course. Perhaps it will be as simple as stepping over a block and then going under the table. Ask them to add one new element at a time to the obstacle course. For example: step over the block, go under the table, and then through the tunnel. Draw a map of the obstacle course.

CONNECT WITH FAMILIES

Display *My Map Book* with the idea chart and Classroom Map. Record some of the questions the children answered in step 6 and display them as well.

Map Your Classroom

After reading *My Map Book*, we made a map of our classroom. We worked hard to include the important things about our room. When we were done, we used the map to help people get from place to place.

When we made and used this map we practiced:

▢ Matching objects to geographical locations,

▢ Using location words such as between, around, next to, and

▢ Using symbols to stand for objects.

See page 193 for a reproducible copy of this note to families.

What's Needed

the book, *My Map Book*

mural paper

construction paper

scissors

glue

tape

markers

discarded magazines (optional)

camera (optional)

Social Studies Standards

People, Places, and Environments

- Using personal experiences as a basis for exploring geographic concepts and skills
- Matching objects to geographical locations
- Mapping
- Using spatial and location words

EXPLORATION:

NEIGHBORHOOD MAP

The children will take a walk in the neighborhood and make a simple picture map to represent the area around the school.

THINGS TO CONSIDER

Plan an interesting and safe walking route around the neighborhood.

Some children may know where objects should go on the map, but may not be able to draw them. They may want to use pictures from magazines to complete their maps.

For children with communication challenges, you may need to use actual photographs of the places on the walk to help them understand that the map represents a place they are familiar with.

STEP BY STEP

1. Engage the children in a conversation about maps. What do they already know about maps? Explain that a map is a picture of a certain area. Maps help us get from one place to another place.

2. Take a short walk around the neighborhood. Stop often and encourage the children to look at and talk about the buildings, trees, signs, roads, parks, and other things they see. Make a list of their observations.

3. When you return, talk together about what you saw, using descriptive and positional words, such as: the blue house was *next to* the store; the store had a sign *above* the door. Refer to the list you made during the walk.

4. Have the children make drawings or paper cutouts to represent each object they want to place on the map. Assist them in deciding where the objects go on the map and then glue or tape them in place. You may wish to add gray construction paper roads and add a photograph of the school.

5. Encourage the children to use the completed map to follow a simple route. They can use a person or animal figure to "walk" on the map and show how someone would get to specific location in the neighborhood.

Talk with Children

On your walk, point out features you want the children to remember. You might say:

Oh, we are on a bridge again. This road goes over the brook twice.

Look how close the school really is to the pond.

SOCIAL STUDIES AND ME!

Remind the children of things they saw on the walk. You might say something like: *I see you put the trees next to the post office. I also remember that there was a parking lot next to the post office. What else do you remember that was near the post office?*

When children make drawings of objects or features that you don't recognize, say: *Tell me about your drawing.* Always respect the intent of their drawings.

Encourage the children to share any personal experiences they have with the area you are mapping. For example, they may play in the area or walk this same route with their families.

Observe Children

O Notice if the children use some of the language of map making and travel in their free play, such as *leads to, next to, past, over, under, next to, across from, near, far.*

O Do any of the children show interest in drawing more maps on their own?

O Do the children use the block area to build three-dimensional maps?

EXTEND THE LEARNING

Challenge the children to make their own maps. Go for another walk following the same route. Talk together about what you notice. Encourage them to make treasure maps or other maps in dramatic play.

Try some of the other mapping ideas from *My Map Book*. Children may enjoy making maps of their hearts, dogs, cats, daily schedules, stomachs, or faces. Encourage creativity in thinking of other things to map.

The children can draw maps of the obstacle course.

CONNECT WITH FAMILIES

Encourage families to celebrate the knowledge their children have gained and the fun they've had while studying maps and mapmaking. Display *My Map Book* near your bulletin board with the neighborhood map and any other maps children have created. Post the following for families to read:

Map Your Neighborhood

We've been exploring *My Map Book* and learning how to make maps. In order to know the neighborhood, we went on a walk and made a map of our route. We learned that maps are special pictures that represent a place. When we made maps, we practiced:

- Using our personal experiences to explore concepts about places,
- Using locational words such as *around, next to, behind,* and
- Following a map to get from one place to another.

See page 193 for a reproducible copy of this note to families.

Vocabulary

globe: a spherical representation of the earth

my country: the land of a person's birth, residence, or citizenship

non-fiction: writing that is about real people, places, and events

Social Studies Standards

Culture

O Identifying and comparing the characteristics and behaviors of people in different climates, locations and societies: What is the same? What is different?

BOOK TALK

In a truly multicultural book, brilliant photographs contributed by Peace Corps volunteers and award-winning photographers illustrate a spirited look at the joys and activities shared by children in 40 countries around the world.

GLOBAL CONNECTIONS

O Exploring issues and concerns common to people around the world
O Understanding that there are other nations with different traditions and practices from our own

MAKING CONNECTIONS

Show the children a world map. Say:

This is a map of the whole world.
Here is where we live.
Did you know there are children all over the world, in all these other places?

Continue to show children the map and ask leading questions such as:

Have you heard of any other countries in the world?
Do you think children in China have friends?
Do you think children in other places go to school?

Keep in mind that while it is important to introduce vocabulary like "country," even young elementary children can be unsure of its meaning. Children may refer to Florida or St. Louis or Africa as a country. Keep using the vocabulary without expecting them to understand the political divisions of the planet.

INTRODUCING THE BOOK

Before introducing this book to the children, study the pages called "Being a Kid." These pages clearly show how the book is divided into eight topics: families, school, after-school activities, play, the arts, animals, fun, and friends. All of these topics are related to social studies learning.

Point to and read aloud the book title and names of the authors. Take a picture walk, looking for pictures that give strong clues about what children like to do.

SOCIAL STUDIES AND ME!

READING AND TALKING TOGETHER

O The map in the front of the book helps the children place the photographs geographically.

O The last two pages review the elements found in the book. Read each section, inviting conversation about the children's personal experiences. "Fun," for example, could lead to a discussion of what they think is fun or what they like to do for fun.

O Here are some tips about how reading nonfiction is different from reading fiction to young children:

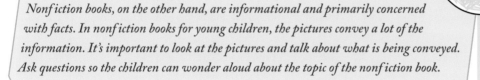

Fiction books are usually stories. They have a beginning, a middle, and an end. They have problems to be solved, drama, and tension. Will the three bears eat Goldilocks? Will anyone ever help the Little Red Hen? Is it possible for Chester and Wilson to be friends with Lily? Because of this tension it is important to read a storybook from beginning to end so that children understand the narrative and the characters' motivation.

Nonfiction books, on the other hand, are informational and primarily concerned with facts. In nonfiction books for young children, the pictures convey a lot of the information. It's important to look at the pictures and talk about what is being conveyed. Ask questions so the children can wonder aloud about the topic of the nonfiction book.

Consider the page in *To Be a Kid* that shows children riding the merry-go-round in Austria. Study the pictures and ask the children questions like these:
What is happening?
What does the picture tell you about Austria?

As you read this section aloud, reflect on what the children learned. Ask:
What did we learn about children in Austria?

What's Needed

the book, *To Be a Kid*
mural paper
markers
paint
paintbrushes
globe or map

Social Studies Standards

Culture

o Identifying and comparing the characteristics and behaviors of people in different climates, locations and societies: What is the same? What is different?

EXPLORATION:

A KID IS A KID IS A KID

Children will use *To Be a Kid* to explore how aspects of childhood can be both similar and different around the world.

GLOBAL CONNECTIONS

o Exploring issues and concerns common to people around the world
o Understanding that there are other nations with different traditions and practices from our own

THINGS TO CONSIDER

When you ask children to discuss similarities and differences between themselves and children in the book, they may mention skin color. Talk about skin color in the same matter-of-fact tone you use for anything else. If adults talk about differences in clothing and homes, but gloss over what children notice about skin color, that sends a powerful message. When differences are not acknowledged, they are magnified and begin to seem mysterious or off limits. This is an invaluable opportunity for you to model acceptance of and respect for differences.

Some children will find spatial relationships easier to see on a globe, some on a flat map. Use both your globe and the map in the book during this exploration.

STEP BY STEP

1. The first section of *To Be a Kid* is about families and what they do together. As you look at those pictures with children, ask:
   What do you notice in the pictures?
   What is the same about all the families?
   Be sure to use accurate social studies language such as, the country of Senegal, the continent of Africa, and the country of the United States.

2. Make connections between what the children in the pictures are doing and the experiences of the children in your group.

3. Identify the country where the picture was taken, and find it on a map. Say:
   This family comes from Portugal. Let's find exactly where they live on the map or globe.
   Repeat with other sections of the book.

SOCIAL STUDIES AND ME!

4 . Title a mural "A Kid Is a Kid Is a Kid…" and record children's comments.

Fritzwa rides on her daddy's shoulders when they go to a parade.
Shoshanna likes to help her Grandpa in his garden.

5. Have the children paint the mural, showing themselves along with children from other countries engaged in fun activities like riding bikes, singing, and dancing.

Talk with Children

Some of the children may have more familiarity than others with countries other than the United States. Ask them what they notice about clothes, or about what the children in the pictures are doing. What is the same and what is different?

Observe Children

O Do the children notice details in the pictures?
O Are they interested in how the globe or the map "works?"
O In what ways do the children demonstrate interest in settings and activities that are different from their own?

EXTEND THE LEARNING

As you go through the book and identify pictures from a variety of countries, photocopy the map from *To Be a Kid* (or use your own world map). Post the map on the wall and mark the countries you have talked about.

Learn songs from other countries, such as:

"Frère Jacques"—France "Grand Old Duke of York"—England
 "Zum Gali Gali"—Israel "La Cucaracha"—Mexico
"Kookaburra"—Australia "Sarasponda"—Ireland

CONNECT WITH FAMILIES

Display *To Be a Kid* together with your globe or world map. Tell the families that the class has been exploring how children in other parts of the world are the same and different from themselves. Post the following:

A Kid Is a Kid Is a Kid

We have been using *To Be a Kid* to see how children all over the world are alike and different. We've been looking at how children in other countries play, spend time with their families, and go to school. We found the countries on the map and globe. We have:

□ Compared characteristics and behaviors of people in different counties,
□ Learned that there are different nations with different traditions and practices, and
□ Explored what activities are common to people around the world.

See page 194 for a reproducible copy of this note to families.

What's Needed

the book, *To Be a Kid*
globe beach ball

Social Studies Standards

People, Places, and Environments

o Matching objects to geographic locations

o Mapping

EXPLORATION:

GLOBE TOSS!

In this introduction to the globe, children will learn to recognize water and land masses.

THINGS TO CONSIDER

A globe, like all maps, is an abstraction. The goal of this exploration for young children is exposure rather than concept mastery.

Look for globe beach balls at your local school supply store or discount department store. If you cannot find an inflatable globe, make one. Inflate a solid blue beach ball. Use acrylic paints to paint large brown "land masses" on the "globe."

You will need a space where children can comfortably stand in a circle and play catch with the globe.

STEP BY STEP

1. Look through *To Be a Kid* with your group. Explain that the children in the book are growing up all over the world, not just near where you live.

2. Show the children the inflated globe. Ask: *What do you think this is?* Listen carefully to what children say and build on their ideas to define the word "globe."

3. Find on the globe some of the places where children in the book live. Find where you live on the globe. Explain that countries are labeled so you can find them. Show them that water (ocean) is blue on the globe and land is another color (usually brown or green).

SOCIAL STUDIES AND ME!

4. Have the children stand in a circle to play catch with the inflatable globe beach ball. To avoid a free-for-all, make sure you give the children clear ground rules. The children should announce the name of the child they are throwing to. For example: *Rachael, are you ready?*

When the child catches the globe, she looks at her thumbs and announces if they are on land or water: *This thumb is on the blue part. It's on the water!*

For some groups, it may work better to sit in a big circle and roll the globe rather than throwing it.

Talk with Children

As the children are talking about maps, challenge them to think about how we might use a globe.

Encourage the children to use location words:
My thumb is on the land but near the water.
The water is at the top of my thumb.
My thumb is next to China!

Encourage the children to think about themselves in relation to the children in the book. You might ask:
Have you ridden a merry-go-round?
Just yesterday Dmitri painted a beautiful picture.
What games do you like to play with a ball?

Observe Children

- Do the children focus on the details of the globe?
- Do they identify the land and water areas appropriately?
- Do any of the children have prior knowledge of maps and globes?

EXTEND THE LEARNING

When this exploration is finished, don't put away the globe. Refer to it often as opportunities arise. If children mention a world event they heard about on TV, show them where it happened on the globe. Show them where Grandma went on vacation. Show them where other books you read take place. Show them what country your snack recipe originated in.

Encourage the children to incorporate maps into their dramatic play. Provide paper so they can draw treasure maps or a map to help friends find the picnic that is happening in the dress-up area.

My Map Book (see pages 134–139) offers more examples of child-centered mapping ideas.

CONNECT WITH FAMILIES

Display *To Be a Kid* with the globe and photos of the children playing catch where families can see them.

Post the following on your bulletin board:

Globe Toss!

We read *To Be a Kid* and looked at a globe to find some of the places the children in the book live. We played a game called "Globe Toss!" and we practiced recognizing land and water on the globe.

We also learned that:

- A globe is a kind of a map,
- A globe is like a picture of the whole world,
- Different places on the globe are labeled with words,
- Water (oceans and seas) is blue on the globe, and
- Land is other colors on the globe.

See page 194 for a reproducible copy of this note to families.

Book Talk

Manyoni lives in the African country of Zimbabwe. Each morning she encounters several wild animals as she sets off past the gray baobab tree, across the fever tree pan, over the krantz above the dam, across the hot plains, and to the village school.

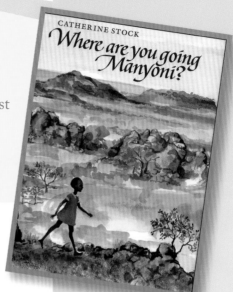

MAKING CONNECTIONS

Engage the children in a conversation about walks they have taken. Ask:

What are some reasons for going on a walk?

Have you ever gone on a walk?

Where did you walk?

What was your reason for going?

What interesting things did you see? Animals? Plants? Buildings? People?

INTRODUCING THE BOOK

Before you read *Where are you going Manyoni?*, use the globe to show the children where Manyoni lives. Explain that the country of Zimbabwe is on the continent of Africa. Talk about the cover and ask:

What can you tell about the weather from this picture?

How does it look the same as where we live? How is it different?

Where do you think Manyoni is going?

Do a picture walk to look at Manyoni's journey, but do not give the final destination away. Read the book aloud to find out where the journey ends.

READING AND TALKING TOGETHER

o After reading the book, engage the children in conversation by asking:

What are some of the things you have in common with Manyoni?

What are some of the things that are different?

Make a chart:

Different from Manyoni	Same as Manyoni

Vocabulary

See the "Unfamiliar Word List" at the back of *Where Are You Going Manyoni?*

Social Studies Standards

Culture

o Recognizing and exploring similarities and differences among individuals' and groups' beliefs, attitudes, and behaviors

Global Connections

o Exploring issues and concerns common to people around the world

○ Read the book again. Show the children the "Wildlife in This Book" section at the back of the book. Explain that the author has given us additional information about the animals Manyoni passes on her walk. Use this information to find and name the animals on each page.

○ Share the cave paintings on the endpapers. Note: in the "Author's Note" at the back of the book you will find more information for this discussion.

SOCIAL STUDIES AND ME!

EXPLORATION:

GETTING-TO-SCHOOL GRAPH

In this exploration children will talk about the different ways they go to school, collect data, and compare their experiences with Manyoni's.

What's Needed
the book, *Where Are You Going Manyoni?*
chart paper
markers
name cards

Social Studies Standards
Culture
O Recognizing and exploring similarities and differences among individuals' and groups' beliefs, attitudes, and behaviors

Global Connections
O Exploring issues and concerns common to people around the world

THINGS TO CONSIDER

This exploration can be repeated over several days or it can become a regular part of the routine of arriving at school.

STEP BY STEP

1. Reread *Where Are You Going Manyoni?* Talk about how Manyoni got to school.

2. Create a chart to show the many ways children get to school. Write a word or draw a symbol for each mode of transportation. Ask each child how he got to school that day and invite him to put his name card in the column where it belongs. When all the name cards are on the graph, ask: What do you notice about our chart today?

	walk	bike	bus	car
Alex				
Brianna				
Courtney				
Charlie				
Devon				

3. Explain that your group will update this chart every day to see how everyone came to school.

4. Update the chart each day, inviting the children to move their name cards to new columns, if necessary. Encourage each child to talk about the change, saying something like: *Yesterday, I took the bus to school, but today I rode in a car with my Mom.*

Talk with Children

As you do this Exploration, remind the children what each symbol represents on the graph.

Children of all ages and developmental stages can participate. If necessary, you can move a child's card, or the child can ask a classmate to do it.

Talk about how the graph might look if Manyoni's class created it. Set out materials and let interested children make a graph to show the result for Manyoni's class in Zimbabwe.

Observe Children

O When children talk about how Manyoni gets to school, what does this tell you about their knowledge of Africa?

O Does the behavior of animals and people in the story differ from what children in your group expected? If so, in what ways?

EXTEND THE LEARNING

Sing a song as you update your chart. Sing to the tune of "Mulberry Bush."

This is the way we ride to school,
Ride to school, ride to school.
This is the way we ride to school,
So early in the morning.

Sing this several times, substituting the way each child gets to school for the word ride. Make up movements to go with each method of getting to school.

CONNECT WITH FAMILIES

Display the transportation graph and the book, *Where Are You Going Manyoni?* where families can see them. Add to the display a note to the parents describing the learning take has taken place.

Getting to School

We read *Where Are You Going Manyoni?* and discovered that Manyoni walks a long distance, passing wild animals, on her way to school every day. It made us think about the different ways we get to school. We made a graph of our findings and we update it every morning. By doing this exploration, we learned that there are many ways to get to school.

See page 195 for a reproducible copy of this note to families.

EXPLORATION:

SAME AND DIFFERENT ROUTINES

Children will discuss the different routines in their daily lives and make a book comparing their routines to each other's and to Manyoni's.

The Big World

What's Needed
the book, *Where Are You Going Manyoni?*
writing paper
crayons
hole punch
yarn

Social Studies Standards
Global Connections
O Exploring issues and concerns common to people around the world

Time, Continuity, and Change
O Gaining experience with sequencing to establish a sense of order and time

Culture
O Identifying and comparing the characteristics and behaviors of people in different climates, locations, and societies: What is the same? What is different?

THINGS TO CONSIDER

Some children will need assistance to work on their pages. Depending on the number of children and adult helpers in your group, bookmaking may have to take place over several days.

When acting out the story, go to an open area where the children have room to move as they dramatize the long journey to the village school.

STEP BY STEP

1. Look through the pages of *Where Are You Going Manyoni?* Ask:
   What is Manyoni's favorite time of day? How do we know?
   What does Manyoni eat for breakfast?

2. Ask the group to act out Manyoni's morning and her walk to school.

3. Ask the children, Do you do the same things every morning? Explain that a routine is something you do over and over. Let them share their morning routines. Tell them you are going to make a book about their routines and Manyoni's routine.

4. Divide the children into small groups. Each group will make several pages for the book. For example: One group can make a "We All Eat Breakfast" section.
   Susan eats a sandwich.   *Justin eats a hot dog.*
   Rachael likes soup.   *Manyoni loves her mother's porridge.*

   The children can choose what to write and then illustrate it. Other sections could be "We All Go to School" or "Some of Us Have Sisters or Brothers."

5. Challenge the children to think of characters in other books that they could include. Hetty in *Down the Road* walks to town. Officer Buckle drives a police car around town and has Gloria as a pet.

6. Bind all of the children's pages together into a book and read it to the group.

Talk With Children

Be clear as you ask the children about Manyoni's morning routine and her walk to school. Ask: *What happens first? What does she see next? What does she see after that?*

Keep pointing out the similarities and the differences between your group and Manyoni. Say: *We all eat, but we like to eat different things.*
We all have people who care for us, but they are different people.
Juanita puts on her boots before her hat, and Amber puts on her hat before her boots. They are both bundled up, but they did it differently.

Observe Children

○ Are the children comfortable making comparisons among multiple characters or people?
○ Which children are eager to share the routines they have at home? Which are reticent about that?
○ Do some children always want to be the "same" as the other children?

EXTEND THE LEARNING

Getting dressed is an activity that children can pantomime and then compare how they do it.

Have the children make a chart to show similarities and differences in their lives as compared to Manyoni's.

Same	Different
We eat breakfast.	We eat toast and Manyoni eats porridge.
We go to school.	Manyoni walks a very long way by herself to school and we take a bus.
We both have roads	Our road is paved and Manyoni's is made of clay.

CONNECT WITH FAMILIES

Celebrate what the children have learned! Display *Where Are You Going Manyoni?*, the book the children made, and the information that follows.

Same and Different Routines

We read *Where Are You Going Manyoni?* and learned that everyone has routines. We made a book about our daily routines. By doing this exploration, we learned:

◘ People have their own routines,

◘ Some of our routines are the same as others' routines, and

◘ Some of our routines are different from others' routines.

See page 195 for a reproducible copy of this note to families.

SOCIAL STUDIES AND ME!

Bibliography

I Am a Person

Aliki. 1989. *My Five Senses*. New York: HarperCollins.
A simple presentation of the five senses, demonstrating ways we use them.

Beaumont, Karen. 2004. *I Like Myself!* Massachusetts: Houghton Mifflin Harcourt.
No matter what anyone else thinks of her, this little girl really likes herself because, as she says, "I'm ME!"

Blegvad, Lenore. 1987. *Anna Banana and Me*. California: Aladdin.
Anna Banana's fearlessness inspires a playmate to face his fears.

Brown, Marc. 1996. *D.W. Rides Again*. New York: Little Brown & Co.
D.W. has graduated from a tricycle to her first two-wheeler and is ready to ride off into the sunset. But first she needs to find out where the brakes are!

Carlson, Nancy L. 2009. *Harriet and the Roller Coaster*. California: Paw Prints.
Harriet accepts her friend George's challenge to ride the frightening roller coaster and finds out that she is the brave one.

Carlstrom, Nancy White. 2010. *Jesse Bear, What Will You Wear?* New York: Simon & Schuster Children's Publishing.
A rhyming text describes Jesse Bear's activities from morning to bedtime.

Chodos-Irvine, Margaret. 2003. *Ella Sarah Gets Dressed*. Massachusetts: Houghton Mifflin Harcourt.
Ella Sarah knows just what she wants to wear. It is not what mom or dad wants, but her stylish friends have similar tastes.

Cooney, Barbara. 1982. *Miss Rumphius*. New York: Penguin Group.
Alice Rumphius loved the sea, longed to visit faraway places, and wished to do something to make the world more beautiful.

Curtis, Jamie Lee. 1996. *Tell Me Again About the Night I Was Born.* New York: HarperCollins.
A young girl asks her parents to tell her again the family story about her birth and adoption.

Curtis, Jamie Lee. 1995. *When I Was Little: A Four-Year-Old's Memoir of Her Youth.* New York: HarperCollins.
A little girl's celebration of herself, as she looks back on her childhood from the lofty height of four-and-a-half years.

Dunbar, Joyce. 2005. *Tell Me What It's Like to Be Big.* London: Sandpiper.
When she wakes up early one morning, Willa questions her big brother about what it will be like to be a grown-up.

Falconer, Ian. 2000. *Olivia.* New York: Atheneum/Anne Schwartz Books.
Whether at home getting ready for the day, enjoying the beach, or at bedtime, Olivia is a feisty pig who has too much energy for her own good.

Falwell, Cathryn. 2005. *David's Drawings.* New York: Lee & Low Books.
A shy African American boy makes friends with his classmates by drawing a picture of a tree.

Feiffer, Jules. 2000. *I Lost My Bear.* New York: HarperCollins.
When she cannot find her favorite stuffed toy, a young girl asks her mother, father, and older sister for help.

Gore, Leonid. 2009. *When I Grow Up.* New York: Scholastic Press.
A little boy wonders what he will be when he grows up. In the end, his greatest inspiration comes from a simple source, his father's love.

Heelan, Jamee Riggio. 2000. *Rolling Along: The Story of Taylor and His Wheelchair.* Georgia: Peachtree.
Taylor, affected by cerebral palsy, gets a wheelchair to help him get around, do things by himself, and even play basketball with his twin, Tyler.

Henkes, Kevin. 1996. *Chrysanthemum.* New York: HarperCollins.
Chrysanthemum loved her name until she went to school and Victoria made fun of it. Things changed when the students met their teacher, Mrs. Delphinium Twinkle.

Henkes, Kevin. 1993. *Owen.* New York: HarperCollins.
Owen's parents try to get him to give up his favorite blanket before he starts school. When their efforts fail, they come up with a solution that makes everyone happy.

Henkes, Kevin. 1996. *Sheila Rae, The Brave*. New York: Greenwillow.
Sheila Rae is the brave one in the family and her sister Louise has always been the scaredy-cat. But one day Sheila Rae gets lost and it is Louise's turn to be the brave one.

Hindley, Judy. 2002. *Eyes, Nose, Fingers and Toes*. Massachusetts: Candlewick Press.
A group of toddlers demonstrate the fun things they can do with their eyes, ears, mouths, hands, legs, feet—and everything in between.

Hoffman, Mary. 1991. *Amazing Grace*. New York: Scholastic Inc.
Grace is determined to be Peter Pan in her school play.

Howard, Arthur. 1999. *When I Was Five.* London: Sandpiper.
A six-year-old boy describes the things he liked when he was five and compares them to the things he likes now.

Hudson, Wade. 1991. *Jamal's Busy Day*. New Jersey: Just Us Books.
A look at young Jamal's busy and successful day.

Hurwitz, Johanna. 1999. *New Shoes for Silvia*. New York: Mulberry Books.
A young girl receives a pair of beautiful red shoes from her Tia Rosita and finds different uses for them until she grows big enough for them to fit.

Hutchins, Pat. 1993. *Titch.* California: Aladdin.
Titch's possessions were always smaller and less significant than his older brother's and sister's, until he planted a seed.

Johnson, Crocket. 1998. *Harold and the Purple Crayon*. New York: HarperCollins.
Harold goes out for a walk with a crayon in his hand and draws himself wonderful adventures.

Kasza, Keiko. 1996. *A Mother for Choco.* New York: Putnam Juvenile.
A lonely little bird named Choco goes in search of a mother.

Keats, Ezra Jack. 1998. *Peter's Chair.* New York: Viking Juvenile.
Peter discovers that his blue furniture is being painted pink for his new baby sister. He decides to take the last unpainted item and run away.

Kraus, Robert. 1994. *Leo the Late Bloomer*. New York: HarperCollins.
Will Leo the Tiger ever bloom? Watch him and find out.

Krauss, Ruth. 2004. *The Carrot Seed*. New York: HarperCollins.
A little boy plants a carrot seed. His mother, father, and big brother agree that it won't come up but the little boy knows better.

Krauss, Ruth. 2007. *The Growing Story*. New York: HarperCollins.
First published in 1947, this classic story celebrates those little changes that tell us we're growing up! Now it blooms again with lush illustrations by one of the world's best-loved illustrators: Helen Oxenbury.

Kuskin, Karla. 2000. *I Am Me*. New York: Simon & Schuster.
After being told how she resembles other members of her family, a young girl states positively that she is "No One Else But Me!"

LaMarche, Jim. 2006. *Up*. California: Chronicle.
Daniel discovers that he can lift objects upward just by concentrating, and his secret power is put to good use when he helps save a beached whale.

Leaf, Munro. 2007. *Story of Ferdinand*. New York: Puffin.
All the other bulls run and jump and butt their heads together. But Ferdinand would rather sit and smell the flowers.

Lester, Helen. 2006. *Tacky the Penguin*. London: Sandpiper.
Tacky the penguin does not fit in with his sleek and graceful companions, but his odd behavior comes in handy when hunters come with maps and traps.

Lewis, Rose A. 2000. *I Love You Like Crazy Cakes*. New York: Little, Brown Young Readers.
A mother's love letter to her adopted Chinese daughter.

London, Jonathan. 1992. *Froggy Gets Dressed*. New York: Puffin.
Rambunctious Froggy hops out into the snow for a winter frolic but is called back by his mother to put on necessary articles of clothing.

McKissack, Patricia. 1986. *Flossie and the Fox*. New York: Dial Books.
A bold little girl insists upon proof of identity from a wily fox before she will be frightened.

Millman, Isaac. 2002. *Moses Goes to a Concert*. New York: Farrar Straus & Giroux.
Moses and his schoolmates, all deaf, attend a concert where the orchestra's percussionist is also deaf.

Mora, Pat. 2010. *Dona Flor*. New York: Dragonfly Books.
Mora's poetic language brings to life this original and engaging character whose love and concern for her neighbors and friends fills the story with joy.

Nikola-Lisa, W. 1995. *Bein' with You This Way*. New York: Lee & Low.
A young girl leads a cumulative rap about individual differences.

SOCIAL STUDIES AND ME!

O'Neill, Alexis. 2002. *The Recess Queen*. New York: Scholastic.
Mean Jean is the bully of the playground. But a new student, Katie Sue, is not at all intimidated by her and they become friends when she asks Mean Jean to play with her.

Pfister, Marcus. 1997. *Penguin Pete*. New York: NorthSouth Books.
Penguin Pete longs for the day when he is big enough to swim with the other penguins.

Phillips, Joan. 1986. *Tiger Is a Scaredy Cat*. New York: Random House.
Tiger, a scaredy cat who is even afraid of the mice in his house, conquers his fear to help Baby Mouse.

Pinkney, Brian. 1997. *Max Found Two Sticks*. New York: Simon & Schuster.
Although he doesn't feel like talking, a young boy responds to questions by drumming on various objects, echoing the city sounds around him.

Pinkney, Jerry. 1999. *The Ugly Duckling*. New York: HarperCollins.
A lovely adaptation of Hans Christian Andersen's classic in which a "duckling" is constantly teased by his supposed siblings because he doesn't look like them. As he grows and transforms, he looks at his reflection in the water and sees that he has become a beautiful swan.

Pinkney, Sandra L. 2000. *Shades of Black: A Celebration of Our Children*. New York: Scholastic Inc.
Photographs and poetic text celebrate the beauty and diversity of African American children.

Piper, Watty. 2005. *The Little Engine That Could*. New York: Philomel.
Taking in the Little Blue Engine's mantra, "I think I can—I think I can," children delight in this classic story of optimistic thinking.

Potter, Beatrix. 2004. *The Tale of Peter Rabbit*. New York: Frederick Warne, Publisher/Penguin Group, USA.
In this classic adventure tale, Peter Rabbit disobeys his mother and has a scary encounter in Mr. McGregor's garden.

Rockwell, Anne. 2001. *Growing Like Me*. Massachusetts: Harcourt Children's Books.
Explains how plants and animals of the meadow, woods, and pond grow and evolve. Caterpillars change into butterflies, eggs hatch into robins, and acorns become oaks.

Sendak, Maurice. 1991. *Where the Wild Things Are*. New York: Scholastic Inc.
Max, sent to bed without his supper, sails to the land of the wild things where he becomes their king.

Seuss, Dr. 2004. *Horton Hatches the Egg*. New York: Random House.
Perseverance pays off for Horton the Elephant as he patiently sits and sits on lazy Maysie's egg while she's off on a (permanent) vacation.

Shannon, David. 1998. *No, David!* New York: Scholastic Inc.
A young boy is depicted doing a variety of forbidden things for which he is repeatedly admonished, but finally he gets a hug.

Urban, Linda. 2009. *Mouse Was Mad*. New York: Houghton Mifflin Harcourt.
Mouse expresses his anger by being very still and quiet, unlike bear who stomps and bobcat who screams. Mouse tries to be like them, but finds that his own way it best for him.

Viorst, Judith. 1972. *Alexander and the Terrible, Horrible, No Good, Very Bad Day*. New York: Scholastic Inc.
Alexander wakes up with gum in his hair. His best friend is mean to him. He has to eat lima beans for dinner. For Alexander, it's a terrible, horrible, no good, very bad day.

Walsh, Melanie. 2002. *My Nose, Your Nose*. Massachusetts: Houghton Mifflin Harcourt.
We have so much in common, and yet we are so different.

Wells, Rosemary. 2000. *Noisy Nora*. New York: Puffin.
Feeling neglected, Nora makes more and more noise to attract her parents' attention.

Wells, Rosemary. 2001. *Shy Charles*. New York: Puffin.
Shy Charles becomes a quiet hero when he saves the day by helping his injured babysitter.

Wells, Rosemary. 2009. *Yoko*. New York: Hyperion.
Yoko's schoolmates make fun of her Japanese sushi at lunchtime.

Willey, Margaret. 2004. *Clever Beatrice*. California: Aladdin.
A spunky girl matches wits with a rich giant in this classic tale of brains versus brawn.

Families

Banks, Kate. 2009. *That's Papa's Way*. New York: Farrar, Straus & Giroux.
Early morning is the perfect opportunity for a little girl and her father to go off fishing and spend some wonderful time together.

SOCIAL STUDIES AND ME!

Bunting, Eve. 1999. *Butterfly House*. New York: Scholastic Inc.
  With her grandfather's help, a little girl makes a house for a larva before setting it free, and every spring butterflies come to visit her.

Burrowes, Adjoa. 2000. *Grandma's Purple Flowers*. New York: Lee & Low.
  A young child finds a way to cope with the death of her beloved grandmother as she discovers a special way to remember her.

Carling, Aelia Lau. 1998. *Mama and Papa Have A Store*. New York: Dial Books.
  A little girl describes what a day is like in her parents' Chinese store in Guatemala City.

Carlson, Nancy. 2001. *How About a Hug?* New York: Viking Press.
  Questions and answers show the reader that different kinds of hugs can be the answer for many situations.

Cisneros, Sandra. 1997. *Hairs – Pelitos*. New York: Dragonfly Books.
  A child describes how each person in his family has hair that looks and acts different.

Corey, Dorothy. 1992. *Will There Be a Lap For Me?* Illinois: Albert Whitman & Co.
  Kyle misses his time on Mother's lap while she is pregnant and is happy when the birth of his baby brother makes her lap available again.

Cowen-Fletcher, Jane. 1993. *Mama Zooms*. New York: Scholastic Inc.
  A boy's mama takes him zooming everywhere with her, because her wheelchair is a zooming machine.

Crews, Donald. 1991. *Bigmama's*. New York: Greenwillow Books.
  Visiting Bigmama's house in the country, young Donald Crews finds his relatives full of news and the old place just the same as the year before.

Cunnane, Kelly. 2006. *For You Are a Kenyan Child*. New York: Schwartz & Wade.
  A gentle story about family, responsibility, and a curious little boy is told through vivid text that highlights the Kenyan countryside and culture.

Dorros, Arthur. 1997. *Abuela*. New York: Penguin Group, USA.
  A girl imagines that she and her grandmother are carried up into the sky and that they can fly over the sights of New York City.

Duncan, Alice Faye. 2005. *Honey Baby Sugar Child*. New York: Simon & Schuster.
  A mother expresses her everlasting love for her child.

Falwell, Catherine. 2008. *Feast for 10*. London: Sandpiper.
  Count from one to ten and then count again.

Fox, Mem. 2000. *Harriet, You'll Drive Me Wild!* Massachusetts: Houghton Mifflin Harcourt.
When a young girl has a series of mishaps at home one Saturday, her mother loses her temper.

Fox, Mem. 1994. *Koala Lou*. Massachusetts: Houghton Mifflin Harcourt.
A young koala, longing to hear her mother speak lovingly to her as she did before other children came along, plans to win back her parent's attention.

Gillard, Denise. 2001. *Music from the Sky*. Canada: Groundwood.
The very special relationship between a girl and her grandfather is captured in this setting of rural Nova Scotia in one of Canada's oldest black communities.

Graham, Bob. 2008. *How to Heal a Broken Wing.* New York: Candlewick.
With the help of his sympathetic mother, Will takes an injured bird home to nurse it back to health, saving a single feather as a good-luck charm for the bird's return to the sky.

Grimes, Nikki. 2006. *Welcome, Precious.* London: Orchard.
A family exultantly welcomes the newest member of their family.

Guy, Ginger Foglesong. *2005. Siesta.* New York: Greenwillow.
A brother and sister and their teddy bear gather items they'll need for their nap/siesta.

Havill, Juanita. 2009. *Jamaica Is Thankful*. Massachusetts: Houghton Mifflin Harcourt.
Jamaica's friend Kristin can't keep her new kitten and hopes that Jamaica will be able to give her a good home, but Jamaica's brother is allergic to cats. In the end the friends realize they should be thankful for everything they already have.

Henkes, Kevin. 1995.*Julius, The Baby of the World*. New York: Greenwillow.
Lily is convinced that the arrival of her new baby brother is the worst thing to happen in their house, until cousin Garland comes to visit.

Hest, Amy. 1995. *In the Rain with Baby Duck*. New York: Candlewick.
Mother Duck is upset because Baby Duck hates the rain, but Grampa Duck reminds Mother that once she had to have an umbrella and little boots too.

Hoban, Russell. 1995. *A Baby Sister for Frances*. New York: HarperFestival.
When a baby sister arrives, Frances the badger finds a charming way to prove her own importance.

Hort, Lenny. 1996. *How Many Stars in the Sky?* New York: William Morrow & Co.
A boy and his father go on a night adventure to count the stars.

SOCIAL STUDIES AND ME!

Jenkins, Emily. 2001. *Five Creatures*. New York: Farrar Straus & Giroux.
A girl describes the three humans and two cats that live in her house, and details some shared traits.

Johnson, Angela. 1992. *Tell Me a Story, Mama*. New York: Scholastic Inc.
A young girl and her mother remember together all the girl's favorite stories about her mother's childhood.

Johnson, Angela. 1993. *When I Am Old with You*. New York: Scholastic Inc.
A small child imagines a future when he will be old with his Grandaddy.

Juster, Norton. 2005. *The Hello, Goodbye Window*. New York: Hyperion.
An overnight visit to Nanna and Poppy is filled with the rituals and love that can make the grandparent-grandchild relationship one of the most special parts of childhood.

Larsen, Andrew. 2009. *The Imaginary Garden*. Canada: Kids Can Press.
Theo and her grandfather miss sitting in the big garden he had before he moved to a new apartment, so they create an imaginary garden.

Lee, Huy Voun.1998. *At the Beach*. New York: Henry Holt.
A mother amuses her young son at the beach by drawing Chinese characters in the sand.

London, Jonathan. 2001. *Froggy Eats Out*. New York: Viking Press.
After Froggy misbehaves at a fancy restaurant, his parents take him to a "fast flies" restaurant to celebrate their anniversary.

Look, Lenore. 2001. *Henry's First Moon Birthday*. New York: Atheneum.
An intergenerational story about a Chinese-American birthday celebration.

Manning, Maurie. 2009. *Kitchen Dance*. New York: Clarion.
A little girl and her brother join their parents in a nighttime dance.

Martin, Bill, et al. 1997. *Knots on a Counting Rope*. New York: Henry Holt.
Boy-Strength-of-Blue-Horses and his grandfather reminisce about the young boy's birth, his first horse, and an exciting horse race.

McCloskey, Robert. 1969. *Make Way for Ducklings*. New York: Scholastic Inc.
Mr. and Mrs. Mallard proudly return to their home in the Boston Public Garden with their eight offspring.

McCloskey, Robert. 1976. *Blueberries for Sal*. New York: Viking Press.
Little Sal and Little Bear both lose their mothers while eating blueberries and almost end up with the other's mother.

Monk, Isabell. 2005. *Family.* Minnesota: First Avenue Editions.
Hope's new dessert blends well with the traditional dishes prepared by her cousins and Aunt Poogee at their annual summer get-together.

Mora, Pat. 1994. *Pablo's Tree.* New York: Simon & Schuster.
A young Mexican American boy looks forward to seeing how his grandfather has decorated the tree he planted on the day the boy was adopted.

Morris, Ann. 2000. *Families.* New York: HarperCollins.
A look at all kinds of families from all over the world.

Mould, Wendy. 2001. *Ants in My Pants.* New York: Clarion Books.
Jacob describes the imaginary animals that are keeping him from getting dressed to go shopping with his mother.

Rattigan, Jama Kim. 1998. *Dumpling Soup.* New York: Little Brown.
A young Hawaiian girl tries to make dumplings for her family's New Year's celebration.

Rylant, Cynthia. 1993. *When I Was Young in the Mountains.* New York: Puffin.
The story of a special Appalachian childhood evokes the love of a place, of a family, and of a way of life.

Schaefer, Lola. 2006. *Toolbox Twins.* New York: Henry Holt.
Cozy pictures depict a father and son sharing time together as they use the implements in their trusty toolboxes.

Scott, Ann. 1996. *On Mother's Lap.* New York: Clarion Books.
A small Eskimo boy discovers that Mother's lap is a very special place with room for everyone.

Sears, Martha; Sears, William; Kelly, Christy Watts. 2001. *Baby on the Way.* New York: Little Brown & Co.
Guides a child expecting a new brother or sister through the waiting process.

Smalls, Irene. 1992. *Jonathan and His Mommy.* New York: Time Warner.
As a mother and son explore their neighborhood, they try various ways of walking.

Smalls, Irene. 1999. *Kevin and His Dad.* New York: Little Brown & Co.
Kevin feels excitement, pride, pleasure, and love as he spends an entire day working and playing with his father.

Smith, Will. 2001. *Just the Two of Us*. New York: Scholastic Inc.
Through the lyrics of Will Smith's hit single, we follow a father and son
relationship through three stages of life.

Soto, Gary. 1996. *Too Many Tamales*. New York: Putnam.
Maria tries on her mother's wedding ring while helping make tamales, then
panics when the ring is missing.

Steig, William. 1998. *Pete's a Pizza*. New York: HarperCollins.
When a rainy day keeps Pete from playing ball outside, his father finds a fun
indoor game to play instead.

Stuvé-Bodeen, Stephanie. 2000. *Mama Elizabeti*. New York: Lee & Low.
Tending her doll is easier for Elizabeti than looking after her new baby sister.

Taulbert, Clifton. 2002. *Little Cliff and the Cold Place*. New York: Dial Books.
Great grandfather Poppa Joe comes up with a plan to give Cliff a firsthand feel
for the Arctic.

Waddell, Martin. 2002. *Can't You Sleep, Little Bear?* Massachusetts: Candlewick.
Terrified of the dark, Little Bear cannot get to sleep, until Big Bear comes up
with a loving and reassuring solution.

Williams, Vera B. 1984. *A Chair for My Mother*. New York: Greenwillow.
A child, her waitress mother, and her grandmother save dimes to buy a
comfortable armchair after all their furniture is lost in a fire.

Williams, Vera B. 1996. *"More More More," Said the Baby*. New York: Greenwillow.
Three babies are given loving attention by a father, grandmother, and mother.

Woodson, Jacqueline. 2000. *Sweet, Sweet Memory*. New York: Hyperion Press.
A child and her grandmother feel sad when Grandpa dies, but as time passes,
funny memories of him make them laugh.

Yaccarino, Dan. 2007. *Every Friday*. New York: Henry Holt.
A father and son share the weekly ritual of walking to the local diner for
breakfast, watching the neighborhood come to life, and urging each other on
from one delightful distraction to another.

Zolotow, Charlotte. 2000. *Do You Know What I'll Do?* New York: HarperCollins.
Portrayal of loving, creative siblings.

Friends

Becker, Bonny. 2008. *A Visitor for Bear.* New York: Walker & Co.
> Bear doesn't like visitors, but a mouse visitor is persistent and just won't go away.

Blegvad, Lenore. 1987. *Anna Banana and Me.* California: Aladdin.
> Anna Banana's fearlessness inspires a playmate to face his fears.

Bottner, Barbara. 1997. *Bootsie Barker Bites.* New York: Putnam.
> Bootsie Barker only wants to play games in which she bites, until one day her friend comes up with a better game.

Caseley, Judith. 2001. *Bully.* New York: Greenwillow Books.
> Mickey has trouble with Jack, a bully at school, until he decides to try being nice to Jack and making him a friend.

Chodos-Irvine, Margaret. 2006. *Best Best Friends.* New York: Houghton Mifflin Harcourt.
> Preschoolers Mary and Clare's friendship is tested on the day of Mary's birthday when she gets lots of attention.

Cohen, Miriam. 2007. *Best Friends.* California: Aladdin.
> After a series of incidents, Jim and Paul's friendship is threatened. But when they band together to help with an emergency in the classroom, they are able to become best friends again.

Dunrea, Olivier. 2002. *Gossie and Gertie.* Massachusetts: Houghton Mifflin Harcourt.
> Gossie and Gertie are best friends. They splash in the rain, play hide-and-seek, and dive in the pond together. Everywhere Gossie goes, Gertie goes, too. Or does she?

Fox, Mem. 1989. *Wilfrid Gordon McDonald Partridge.* California: Kane/Miller Book Publisher.
> A small boy tries to discover the meaning of "memory" so he can restore the memory of an elderly friend.

Freeman, Don. 2008. *Corduroy.* New York: Viking Juvenile.
> Corduroy the bear takes a tour of a department store while looking for his missing button.

Havill, Juanita. 1995. *Jamaica's Blue Marker.* Massachusetts: Houghton Mifflin Harcourt.
> Jamaica thinks her classmate Russell is a pest, but then she discovers he is moving away.

Henkes, Kevin. 1996. *Chrysanthemum*. New York: HarperCollins.
Chrysanthemum loved her name until she went to school where Victoria made fun of it. Nothing got better until they met their music teacher, Mrs. Delphinium Twinkle.

Henkes, Kevin. 1998. *Jessica*. New York: Greenwillow.
Ruthie insists on bringing her imaginary friend, Jessica, with her on her first day in kindergarten, though her parents try to persuade her otherwise. Ruthie prevails, only to discover a real friend named Jessica in her class.

Hest, Amy. *2008. The Dog Who Belonged to No One*. New York: Abrams.
A small homeless dog with crooked ears, and a little girl who pedals her bicycle alone, delivering breads and cakes, both dream of finding a friend. When fate brings them together, they discover how they belong to each other.

Hoban, Russell. 2009. *Best Friends for Frances*. New York: HarperCollins.
When Albert and his buddies have a "no girls" baseball game, Frances and her sister organize a "Best Friends Outing – No Boys."

Howe, James. 1999. *Horace and Morris but Mostly Dolores*. New York: Atheneum.
Three mouse friends learn that the best clubs include everyone.

Hutchins, Pat. 1993. *My Best Friend*. New York: HarperCollins.
A girl describes all the things her best friend can do well. When they share a sleepover we see who can really do things best.

Isadora, Rachel. 2009. *Happy Belly, Happy Smile*. Massachusetts: Houghton Mifflin Harcourt.
Louie's grandpa owns a Chinese restaurant. Louie goes there every Friday night to visit the chefs, watch the hustle and bustle, and eat his favorite food. What's *your* favorite dish?

Johnson, D. B. 2000. *Henry Hikes to Fitchburg*. Massachusetts: Houghton Mifflin Harcourt.
While his friend works to earn the train fare to Fitchburg, young Henry walks the thirty miles through woods and fields, enjoying nature.

Keats, Ezra Jack. 1998. *Goggles!* New York: Puffin.
Two boys must outsmart the neighborhood bullies before they can enjoy their new treasure, a pair of lenseless motorcycle goggles.

Lobel, Arnold. 1990. *Frog and Toad Are Friends*. New York: HarperFestival.
Whether telling stories, taking walks, or writing letters, Frog and Toad always help each other out.

Long, Loren. 2009. *Otis.* New York: Philomel.

    Otis is a happy, friendly little tractor—until the farmer brings home a shiny big new yellow tractor. Otis ends up in the weeds behind the shed, feeling left out and indifferent to his former friends. But when Otis pulls his friend Calf out of Mud Pond, he becomes a hero and finds his niche on the farm.

Marshall, James. 1974. *George and Martha.* London: Sandpiper.

    Two lovable hippos demonstrate the meaning of friendship in five engaging vignettes.

Naylor, Phyllis Reynolds. 1994. *The King of the Playground.* California: Aladdin.

    Kevin loves to go to the playground, but not when Sammy is there. Sammy says he will do awful, terrible things to him.

Peguero, Leone. 1996. *Lionel and Amelia.* New York: Mondo Publishing.

    Lionel is a very tidy mouse. Amelia is quite messy. And being friends is easy, as long as they both stay true to themselves.

Perkins, Lynne Rae. 1995. *Home Lovely.* New York: HarperCollins.

    Tiffany transplants and cares for some seedlings she has found and is surprised by what they become.

Raschka, Chris. 2007. *Yo! Yes?* New York: Scholastic Inc.

    Two lonely characters meet on the street and become friends.

Reiser, Lynn. 1993. *Margaret and Margarita.* New York: Mulberry Books.

    Margaret speaks only English, and Margarita speaks only Spanish. They meet in the park and have fun playing even though they have different languages.

Seeger, Laura Vaccaro. 2007. *Dog and Bear.* New York: Roaring Brook Press.

    Three clever little vignettes illustrate the joys of having a best friend at your side as they tell of the misadventures of two unlikely pals – brave, boisterous Dog and shy Bear.

Silverman, Erica. *Don't Fidget a Feather.* Colorado: Sagebrush.

    Two competitive waterfowl have a freeze-in-place contest until a fox happens by.

Steig, William. 2010. *Doctor DeSoto.* New York: Square Fish Books.

    Delightful Doctor DeSoto handles all his patients with care until he meets a new client, the wily fox.

Willems, Mo. 2008. *I Love My New Toy!* New York: Hyperion.
  Piggie has a great new toy though she's not exactly sure what it does. Elephant thinks it's a throwing toy. Throw it he does and it smashes into two pieces. This threatens their friendship until Squirrel comes along and sees that it's a "break-and-snap" toy and still as good as new. They soon realize that playing together is more fun than any old toy.

Willems, Mo. 2004. *Knuffle Bunny.* New York: Hyperion.
  Using a combination of Brooklyn neighborhood photos and illustrated characters, Mo Willems takes readers along on an errand. Even a trip to the laundromat can be an exciting adventure for a toddler…not to mention for a bunny.

Woodson, Jacqueline. 2001. *The Other Side*. New York: Putnam.
  Two girls, one white and one black, gradually get to know each other as they sit on the fence that divides their town.

Communities

Adler, David A. 2009. *Money Madness*. New York: Holiday House.
  A colorful introduction to basic economics.

Aston, Dianne Hutts. 2007. *An Orange in January*. New York: Dial Books.
  Follow an orange as it travels from orchard to consumer in this basic lesson on economics.

Banks, Kate. 2000. *The Night Worker*. New York: Farrar Straus & Giroux.
  Alex wants to be a "night worker" like his father who works at a construction site after Alex goes to bed.

Barber, Barbara. 1996. *Saturday at The New You*. New York: Lee & Low.
  Shauna, a young African American girl, wants to help Momma with the customers at her beauty salon. One day she gets her chance.

Barracca, Debra. 2000. *The Adventures of Taxi Dog*. New York: Puffin.
  The driver of a Checker cab adopts Maxi, a stray dog, and takes him along on his daily rounds.

Barton, Byron. 1987. *Machines at Work*. New York: HarperCollins.
  During a busy day at the construction site, the workers use a variety of machines to knock down a building and begin constructing a new one.

Barton, Byron. 1987. *Airport*. New York: HarperTrophy.
  From the excitement of arrival to the wonder of taking off, the magic of an airport is captured.

Barton, Byron. 1992. *I Want to Be an Astronaut.* New York: HarperCollins.
    All about astronauts as they work, eat and sleep aboard the space shuttle.

Barton, Byron. 1994. *The Little Red Hen*. New York: Harper Festival.
    The little red hen finds none of her lazy friends willing to help her plant, harvest or grind wheat into flour, but all are eager to eat the bread she makes from it.

Blos, Joan W. 1990. *Old Henry.* New York: HarperCollins.
    Henry's neighbors are scandalized that he ignores them and lets his property get run down, until they drive him away and find they miss him.

Brisson, Pat. 1995. *Benny's Pennies*. New York: Yearling Books.
    When Benny wonders what to buy with his five new pennies, he receives five different answers from his family.

Brisson, Pat. 2000. *Wanda's Roses.* Pennsylvania: Boyds Mills Press.
    Wanda mistakes a thorn bush for a rosebush in the empty lot. She clears away the trash around it and cares for it every day, even though no roses bloom.

Bullard, Lisa. 2002. *My Neighborhood: Places and Faces (All About Me).* Minnesota: Picture Window.
    Follow Libbie on a tour of her favorite places and people in her neighborhood.

Burton, Virginia Lee. 1974. *Katy and the Big Snow.* London: Sandpiper.
    Katy, a brave and untiring tractor, who pushes a bulldozer in the summer and a snowplow in the winter, makes it possible for the townspeople to do their jobs.

Carle, Eric. 1998. *Walter the Baker*. California: Aladdin.
    By order of the Duke, Walter the baker must invent a tasty roll through which the rising sun can shine three times.

Carling, Aelia Lau. 1998. *Mama and Papa Have a Store*. New York: Dial Books.
    A little girl describes what a day is like in her parents' Chinese store in Guatemala City.

Cocca-Leffler, Maryann. 2000. *Bus Route to Boston*. Pennsylvania: Boyds Mills Press.
    Describes the pleasure of riding a bus to a new and exotic destination.

Collier, Bryan. 2000. *Uptown*. New York: Henry Holt & Co.
    A tour of the sights of Harlem, including the train, brownstones, shopping, a barbershop, summer basketball, the Harlem Boys Choir, and sunset over the Hudson River.

SOCIAL STUDIES AND ME!

Cooper, Elisha. 1999. *Building*. New York: Greenwillow Books.
  Describes the process of construction, step by step, from clearing the site to cleaning up the finished building.

Crews, Nina. 1995. *One Hot Summer Day*. New York: Greenwillow Books.
  Relates a child's activities in the heat of a summer day punctuated by a thunderstorm.

Crews, Nina. 2004. *The Neighborhood Mother Goose.* New York: Amistad.
  Favorite nursery rhymes with a contemporary look.

Cronin, Doreen. 2004. *Duck for President.* New York: Simon & Schuster.
  Duck, tired of doing chores on the farm, has ever higher ambitions and ends up running the country.

Cumpiano, Ina. 2005. *Quinito's Neighborhood/El Vecindario de Quinito.* California: Children's Book Press.
  Quinito not only knows everyone in his neighborhood, he also knows that each person in his community has a different, important occupation.

Dodds, Dayle Ann. 2007. *Minnie's Diner: A Multiplying Menu.* Massachusetts: Candlewick.
  The wonderful aromas from Minnie's diner draw in farmer Papa McFay's sons one by one, each one twice as big and hungry as the last, in this humorous lesson in multiplication.

Gibbons, Gail. 1986. *The Post Office Book: Mail and How It Moves.* New York: HarperCollins.
  Follow a letter as it moves through the mailing process from the mailbox to its final destination.

Greenfield, Eloise. 1991. *Night on Neighborhood Street.* New York: Puffin.
  The magical and the everyday reside comfortably together on Neighborhood Street.

Havill, Juanita. 1999. *Jamaica and the Substitute Teacher*. Massachusetts: Houghton Mifflin Harcourt.
  Jamaica copies her friend's spelling test because she wants a perfect paper, but her substitute teacher Mrs. Duval helps her understand that she doesn't have to be perfect to be special.

Hoban, Lillian. 1987. *Arthur's Loose Tooth*. New York: HarperTrophy.
  Arthur the chimp, who is afraid of his loose tooth, and his little sister learn something about being brave.

Hutchins, Pat. 1989. *The Doorbell Rang*. New York: Greenwillow.
   Each time the doorbell rings, there are more people who have come to share Ma's wonderful cookies.

Kalman, Bobbie. 1997. *Community Helpers from A to Z (Alphabasics)*. New York: Crabtree.
   Meet the people who make our communities cleaner, safer, more pleasant places to live, including agricultural workers, firefighters, recycling workers, and veterinarians.

Kalman, Bobbie. 2000. *What is a Community from A to Z (Alphabasics)*. New York: Crabtree.
   Discusses features common to most communities: culture, people, government, economy, transportation, buildings and services.

Kimmel, Elizabeth Cody. 2007. *The Top Job*. New York: Dutton.
   On Career Day Mrs. Feeny asks her students to share what their parents do for a living. The narrator shares that her dad changes light bulbs. At first she is ridiculed until she tells them that he changes the "tippy top" bulb on the top of the Empire State Building.

Laden, Nina. 2000. *Roberto, the Insect Architect*. California: Chronicle.
   Roberto is determined to become an architect even though the other termites mock him.

Lionni, Leo. 1973. *Swimmy*. New York: Dragonfly.
   When Swimmy is left alone in the ocean, he must devise a clever plan to keep from being eaten.

London, Jonathan. 1995. *Like Butter on Pancakes*. New York: Viking Press.
   As the sun rises and sets, its light highlights simple aspects and situations of farm life.

Markes, Julie. 2004. *Shhhh! Everybody's Sleeping*. New York: HarperCollins.
   Community workers are shown sleeping in their workplaces.

Miranda, Anne. 2001. *To Market, To Market*. London: Sandpiper.
   Starting with the nursery rhyme about buying a fat pig at market, this tale goes on to describe a series of unruly animals that run amok.

Moss, Lloyd. 1995. *Zin! Zin! Zin! A Violin*. New York: Simon & Schuster.
   Written in elegant verse and illustrated with playful, flowing artwork, this unique counting book is the perfect introduction to musical instruments and orchestras.

SOCIAL STUDIES AND ME!

Paulsen, Gary. 1998. *The Tortilla Factory*. London: Sandpiper.
How a tortilla is made, from the planting of corn to the factory.

Rockwell, Anne. 2002. *Career Day*. New York: HarperCollins.
It's Career Day at school and the students introduce their family's careers to their classmates.

Rotner, Shelley. 2003. *Everybody Works.* Connecticut: Millbrook Press.
A simple, upbeat look at the world of work.

Rylant, Cynthia. 1996. *The Bookshop Dog*. New York: Scholastic Inc.
When the owner of Martha Jane's Bookshop goes into the hospital, the whole town fights over who will take care of Martha Jane, the owner's beloved dog.

Seuss, Dr. 1989. *And to Think That I Saw it on Mulberry Street*. New York: Random House.
Marco tells of the fantastical events he sees on his way home from school.

Sis, Peter. 2000. *Madlenka*. New York: Frances Foster Books.
A girl joyfully skips around her New York City block to proclaim the news of a loose tooth.

Sturges, Philemon. 2002. *The Little Red Hen (Makes a Pizza)*. New York: Penguin Group, USA.
When the Little Red Hen spies a can of tomato sauce in her cupboard, she knows it's time to make pizza.

Waber, Bernard. 1996. *Lyle at the Office.* London: Sandpiper.
Lyle, the lovable crocodile, spends time in an advertising office.

Wellington, Monica. 2001. *Apple Farmer Annie*. New York: Dutton Books.
Annie the apple farmer saves her most beautiful apples to sell fresh at the farmer's market.

Willems, Mo. 2003. *Don't Let the Pigeon Drive the Bus!* New York: Hyperion Books for Children.
When a bus driver takes a break from his route, a very unlikely volunteer springs up to take his place—a pigeon!

Williams, Rozanne Lanczak. 2001. *The Coin Counting Book.* Massachusetts: Charlesbridge.
Simple rhymes and photographs instruct children in coin denominations, grouping, and counting.

Wolfe, Frances. 2001. *Where I Live*. New York: Tundra Books.
"Where I Live" is the seaside where the sun winks off the waves, breezes cool the evening, and treasures are waiting to be discovered.

The Big World

Aardema, Verna. 1992. *Bringing the Rain to Kapiti Plain*. New York: Puffin.
A tale about how a villager brings rain to the plains and saves his animals.

Beeler, Selby B. 2001. *Throw Your Tooth on the Roof*. London: Sandpiper.
Tooth traditions around the world.

Blackstone, Stella. 2005. *My Granny Went to Market*. Massachusetts: Barefoot.
Fly away with Granny as she races around the world on a magic carpet, buying all kinds of things from the countries she visits.

Bursik, Rose. 1994. *Amelia's Fantastic Flight*. New York: Henry Holt & Co.
A young girl builds her own airplane and flies around the world before returning home for dinner.

Charles, Faustin. 1996. *A Caribbean Counting Book*. Massachusetts: Houghton Mifflin.
Traditional and contemporary Caribbean counting rhymes, jump-rope chants, and games.

Chen, Chih-Yuan. 2007. *On My Way to Buy Eggs*. New York: Random House.
A Taiwanese girl's imagination soars as she set off on a simple errand. With gentle humor this timeless tall tale demonstrates how children largely live in and appreciate the moment.

Cunnane, Kelly. 2006. *For You Are a Kenyan Child*. New York: Atheneum/Anne Schwartz Books.
A gentle story about family, responsibility, and a curious little boy is told through vivid text that highlights the Kenyan countryside and culture.

De Beer, Hans. 2000. *Little Polar Bear and the Brave Little Hare*. New York: North South Books.
Lars gains a new friend when he saves Hugo, a nervous hare, from a hole. They share adventures and Hugo gets to show his own courage by getting Lars out of a jam.

Demi. 2007. *The Empty Pot*. New York: Henry Holt & Co.
When Ping admits that he is the only child in China unable to grow a flower from the Emperor's seeds, he is rewarded for his honesty.

SOCIAL STUDIES AND ME!

Daikité, Baba Wagué. 1999. *The Hatseller and the Monkeys*. New York: Scholastic Inc.
BaMusa the hatseller travels from town to town with his hats piled high on his head. One day he falls asleep and when he wakes up, his hats are gone.

Evans, Lezlie. 2004. *Can You Count Ten Toes? Count to 10 in 10 Different Languages*. London: Sandpiper Books.
Counting to 10 in 10 languages, including Spanish, Japanese, Russian, Tagalog, and Hebrew.

Feelings, Muriel. 1992. *Jambo Means Hello: Swahili Alphabet Book*. New York: Puffin.
An alphabet book that teaches Swahili words and African culture.

Fine, Edith Hope. 2002. *Under the Lemon Moon*. New York: Lee & Low.
The theft of lemons from her lemon tree leads Rosalinda to an encounter with la Anciana, the Old One, who helps her understand generosity and forgiveness.

Flack, Marjorie. 2000. *The Story About Ping*. New York: Penguin Group, USA.
A little duck finds adventure on the Yangtze River when he is too late to board his master's houseboat one evening.

Fox, Mem. 1997. *Whoever You Are*. London: Sandpiper.
Despite the differences between people around the world, there are similarities that join us together, such as pain, joy, and love.

Garland, Sherry. 1993. *The Lotus Seed*. New York: Voyager.
A young Vietnamese girl saves a lotus seed and carries it with her everywhere to remember a brave emperor and the homeland that she has to flee.

George, Lindsay. 1996. *Around the Pond*. New York: Greenwillow Books.
While picking blueberries on a warm summer afternoon, Cammy and her brother see signs of animals including footprints, a dam, and a floating feather.

Global Fund for Children. 2007. *Global Babies*. Massachusetts: Charlesbridge.
Seventeen cultures, seventeen beautiful babies. Appealing color photographs depict diverse traditions and showcase clothing worn by babies from around the world.

Gollub, Matthew. 2000. *Ten Oni Drummers*. New York: Lee & Low.
One by one, ten tiny oni, Japanese goblin-like creatures, grow larger as they beat their drums on the sand, chasing away bad dreams.

Ho, Minfong. 2000. *Hush!: A Thai Lullaby*. London: Orchard.
A variety of creatures from a mosquito to an elephant come weeping, peeping, creeping and leaping to disturb a Thai baby's sleep. In the end it is the mother who falls asleep.

Hoberman, Mary Ann. 2007. *A House is a House for Me*. New York: Puffin.
  Lists in rhyme the dwellings of various animals and things.

Hoffman, Mary. 1995. *Boundless Grace*. New York: Scholastic Inc.
  A little girl goes to visit her family in Africa.

Isadora, Rachel. 1994. *At the Crossroads*. New York: Greenwillow.
  South African children gather to welcome home their fathers who have been
  away for several months working in the mines.

Jonas, Ann. 1992. *Round Trip*. California: Live Oak Press.
  Black and white illustrations and text record the sights on a day trip to the city
  and back home again to the country.

Katz, Karen. 1999. *The Colors of Us.* New York: Henry Holt & Co.
  Seven-year-old Lena and her mother observe the variations in the color of their
  friends' skin, viewed in terms of food and things found in nature.

Kimmel, Eric A. 2004. *Anansi and the Talking Melon*. California: Live Oak.
  A clever spider tricks Elephant and some other animals into thinking the melon
  in which he is hiding can talk.

Kurtz, Jane. 1998. *Storyteller's Beads*. Massachusetts: Houghton Mifflin Harcourt.
  During the political strife and famine of the 1980s, two Ethiopian girls struggle
  to overcome many difficulties as they make the dangerous journey out of
  Ethiopia.

Lee, Huy Voun. 1998. *At the Beach*. New York: Henry Holt & Co.
  A mother amuses her young son at the beach by drawing in the sand Chinese
  characters, many of which resemble the objects they stand for.

Lin, Grace. 2009. *The Ugly Vegetables*. Massachusetts: Charlesbridge Publishing.
  A little girl thinks her mother's garden is the ugliest in the neighborhood until
  she discovers that flowers might be pretty, but Chinese vegetable soup smells
  best.

McDermott, Gerald. 2005. *Jabuti the Tortoise: A Trickster Tale from the Amazon*.
  London: Sandpiper.
  All the birds enjoy the song-like flute music of Jabuti, the tortoise, except
  Vulture who tricks Jabuti into riding on his back.

Morales, Yuji. 2003. *Just a Minute: A Trickster Tale and Counting Book*.
  California: Chronicle.
  When Senor Calavera, or death, comes to take Grandma Beetle, she tricks them
  with a "just a minute" response. Text in English and Spanish.

Morris, Ann. 1993. *Bread Bread Bread.* New York: HarperCollins.
  Photographs showing different types of bread from all over the world.

Morris, Ann. 1995. *Houses and Homes.* New York: HarperTrophy.
  A photographic survey of housing around the world.

Morris, Ann. 1994. *On the Go.* New York: HarperCollins.
  People around the world travel in many ways – we walk and run, ride on animals, and use wheels and boats to get us from place to place.

Moss, Miriam. 2005. *This is the Oasis.* California: Kane/Miller Books.
  Lyrical description of the ancient Baobab tree and how it provides shelter and nourishment to wildlife of the African plain.

Musgrove, Margaret. 2001. *The Spider Weaver: A Legend of Kente Cloth.* New York: Scholastic Inc.
  The story of how a beautiful spider shared her weaving secrets with two resourceful, expert weavers.

O'Neill, Alexis. 2002. *Estela's Swap.* New York: Lee & Low.
  A young Mexican American girl accompanies her father to a swap meet, where she hopes to sell her music box for money for dancing lessons.

Onyefulu, Ifeoma. 1997. *A is for Africa.* New York: Puffin.
  The author, a member of the Igbo tribe in Nigeria, presents text and her own photographs of twenty-six things, from A to Z, representative of different African peoples.

Pellegrini, Nina. 1991. *Families Are Different.* New York: Holiday House.
  Korean-born Nico doesn't like looking different from her adoptive parents, but her mother reassures here that there are lots of different kinds of families all "glued together with a special kind of glue called love."

Priceman, Marjorie. 1996. *How to Make an Apple Pie and See the World.* New York: Dragonfly Books.
  Since the market is closed, the reader is led around the world to gather the ingredients for making an apple pie.

Ringgold, Faith. 1996. *Tar Beach.* New York: Dragonfly Books.
  A young girl dreams of flying above her Harlem home, claiming all she sees for herself and her family.

Rockwell, Anne. 2000. *Our Earth.* London: Sandpiper.
  An introduction to geography including how the earth was shaped, how islands are born from volcanoes, and how gushing springs affect rivers.

Rosen, Michael J. 2006. *Chanukah Lights Everywhere*. London: Sandpiper.
    A boy counts the candles on the family menorah and the lights he sees in the world around him on each night of Hanukkah.

Rotner, Shelley. 2009. *Shades of People*. New York: Holiday House.
    Coca, tan rose, and almond – people come in lots of shades, even in the same family. This exploration of one of our most visible physical traits uses vibrant photographs of children to inspire young children both to take notice and to look beyond the obvious.

Rylant, Cynthia. 1991. *Night in the Country*. California: Aladdin.
    Describes the sights and sounds of nighttime in the country.

Schaefer, Carole Lexa. 1999. *The Squiggle*. New York: Dragonfly.
    A young girl finds a piece of string which her imagination turns into a dragon's tail, an acrobat, fireworks, a storm cloud, and more.

Seeger, Pete. 2001. *Abiyoyo*. New York: Simon & Schuster Children's Publishing.
    After their town has ostracized them, a South African boy and his father rescue the townspeople from a marauding giant.

Seeger, Pete. 2004. *Abiyoyo Returns*. New York: Aladdin.
    A South African tale of a giant who, banished from a town thirty years earlier, is called back to save the town from flooding.

Singer, Marilyn. 2000. *On the Same Day in March—A Tour of the World's Weather*. New York: HarperCollins.
    Highlights a wide variety of weather conditions by taking a tour around the world one March day.

Stock, Catherine. 1993. *Where Are You Going Manyoni?* New York: HarperCollins.
    A young girl sees wild birds and other animals on the walk to school. Set in the African country of Zimbabwe.

Stuvé-Bodeen, Stephanie. 2002. *Elizabeti's Doll*. New York: Lee & Low.
    When a young Tanzanian girl gets a new baby brother she finds a rock, which she names Eva, and makes it her baby doll.

Swamp, Chief Jake. 1997. *Giving Thanks: A Native American Good Morning Message*. New York: Lee & Low.
    A Mohawk message of gratitude for the natural world.

SOCIAL STUDIES AND ME!

Thong, Roseanne. 2000. *Round is a Mooncake: A Book of Shapes.* California: Chronicle.
As a little girl discovers things round, square, and rectangular in her urban neighborhood, she is reminded of her Chinese American culture.

Torres, Leyla. 1999. *Saturday Sancocho.* New York: Farrar, Straus and Giroux.
Maria Lilli and her grandparents only have eggs and have run out of money, but they still want to make their usual Saturday chicken stew (*sancocho*). They bring their eggs to the market, bartering their goods until they have all the ingredients they need.

Waboose, Jan Bourdeau. 1997. *Morning on the Lake.* New York: Kids Can Press.
During a canoe outing with his grandfather, a young boy gradually comes to respect the ways of nature and understand his own place in the world.

Walters, Virginia. 2002. *Are We There Yet Daddy?* New York: Puffin Books.
Every time a little boy asks his Dad, "Are we there yet?" his Dad tells him to look at the map.

Williams, Sherley Anne. 1997. *Working Cotton.* London: Sandpiper.
A young girl relates the daily events of her family's migrant life in the cotton fields of central California.

Winter, Jeannette. 2007. *Angelina's Island.* New York: Farrar, Straus and Giroux.
Angelina dreams of home in Jamaica and longs for island food, friends, and family. Then she joins in activities for the annual Carnival parade and finds a bit of her beloved Caribbean island in the Brooklyn sun.

Young, Ed. 2004. *The Lost Horse: A Chinese Folktale.* London: Sandpiper.
In this retelling of an ancient Chinese folktale, Sai, the wise man explains that things are neither as good nor as bad as they seem.

FOR FAMILIES

Book reference: *I'm Growing!* by Aliki

What we are learning…
Talking about growing helps us explore social studies ideas like remembering the past and comparing how we change and grow, and how each of us has different strengths and challenges, likes and dislikes.

Making an "I'm Growing!" Book

We've been talking about all the things babies can do and all the things bigger children can do. We tried to remember some of the things we did when we were babies and then we told what we could do now that we're growing! We used this information to make an "I'm Growing!" book.

FOR FAMILIES

Book reference: *I'm Growing!* by Aliki

What we are learning…

Dear Families,

We've been using non-standard units of measure to help us see just how tall we really are. This helped us understand and describe one of our physical characteristics and to talk about ways we are the same and different.

You can keep track of your child's growth by marking his height on a door or on a piece of paper taped to a wall. Make it more fun by recording the heights of every family member!

FOR FAMILIES

Book reference: *Cleversticks* by Bernard Ashley, Illustrated by Derek Brazell

What we are learning…

I Can Do It!

We've been learning about how people use tools to make their work easier. We explored real tools and sorted them by the jobs they do. We learned that:

- People create or invent tools to do specific jobs,
- Some tools can do more than one job, and
- Sometimes different tools can do similar jobs.

FOR FAMILIES

Book reference: *Cleversticks* by Bernard Ashley, Illustrated by Derek Brazell

What we are learning…

Everyone Is an Expert

Inspired by Ling Sung in the book *Cleversticks,* we talked about all of the things we are experts at. Each child made a page in our class book to illustrate their expertise. We will add to our book later in the year to see how we have grown and changed. Things we talked about:

- Everyone is good at something,
- People have to practice a lot before they become an expert at something,
- Different people are experts at different things, and
- As people grow and change, they learn new skills and become experts at new things.

FOR FAMILIES

Book reference: *Sometimes I'm Bombaloo* by Rachel Vail, Illustrated by Yumi Heo
What we are learning…

Self-Portrait

After reading *Sometimes I'm Bombaloo*, we took time to look carefully at our faces in a mirror and drew what we saw. We talked about:

- The parts of our faces,
- How our features are the same and different,
- What we especially like about how we look, and
- What our faces can tell others about how we feel.

FOR FAMILIES

Book reference: *Sometimes I'm Bombaloo* by Rachel Vail, Illustrated by Yumi Heo
What we are learning…

Making Feelings Masks

After we read *Sometimes I'm Bombaloo* we talked about different feelings we have and how they can show on our faces. We made masks to show these different feelings. We learned to:

- Identify lots of different feelings like sad, surprised, happy, and scared,
- Make faces to show these feelings,
- Make a mask to show a feeling, and
- Act out feelings using the masks.

How Do You Zoom?

We read *Mama Zooms*, a book about a mother who takes her son everywhere in her zooming machine, which is really a wheelchair. To help children learn more about what life is like for people with different physical abilities, we played a game called "Zoom Challenge." In the game we tried to do things like move across the classroom using only one foot, or build with blocks using only one hand. By taking and meeting these challenges, we were able to broaden our understanding of different people's lives and develop empathy for others' experiences. We also spent time thinking and talking about how people invent tools and machines to help accomplish tasks.

FOR FAMILIES

Book reference: *Mama Zooms* by Jane Cowen-Fletcher

What we are learning…

When we read *Mama Zooms* we noticed the family in the book likes to do some of the same things we like to do with our families. We explored what kinds of things all of our families like to do. We learned that:

- Families like to spend time together,
- Families enjoy lots of different things, and
- Families are both very similar and very different.

FOR FAMILIES

Book reference: *I Love Saturdays y domingos* by Alma Flor Ada,
Illustrated by Elivia Savadier
What we are learning…

We Take Care of "Babies"

We've been exploring how families take care of each other. We made baby dolls and practiced caring for them. We learned:

- Adults take care of babies and children,
- Adults do things for babies and children until they are able to do things for themselves,
- People in families take care of each other, and
- It is a lot of work caring for a baby.

FOR FAMILIES

Book reference: *I Love Saturdays y domingos* by Alma Flor Ada,
Illustrated by Elivia Savadier
What we are learning…

What's in a Name?

When we read *I Love Saturdays y domingos* we noticed that the little girl has special names for each of her grandparents. We made pictographs of the names we use for our grandfathers and our grandmothers.

We learned that:

- Grandparents are our parents' parents,
- Families often have special names for grandparents,
- All of our families have similarities, and
- All of our families are different.

FOR FAMILIES

Book reference: *I Love Saturdays y domingos* by Alma Flor Ada,
Illustrated by Elivia Savadier
What we are learning…

Memory Box

Thank you for helping us put together our Memory Boxes. Here is a chart showing
the things that are special to the children because they help bring back memories of
special times, events, or people. In making and sharing Memory Boxes, we:

- Learned about ourselves as individuals and as parts of groups,

- Increased our understanding of each other, and

- Described our own characteristics, especially what we like and care about.

FOR FAMILIES

Book reference: *How Many Stars in the Sky?* by Lenny Hort,
Paintings by James E. Ransome
What we are learning…

Create Your Own Environment

The book *How Many Stars in the Sky?* introduced children to the concepts of city,
town, and countryside. We decided to learn more about _____ and have
created this model to show what it might look like. What features do you notice
that show you the children have learned a lot about this particular place?

Book reference: *Down the Road* by Alice Schertle, Illustrated by E.B. Lewis
What we are learning…

My Family Map

We are learning about families. We all dictated or drew maps of our families.
We learned:

- Families are people who love you,
- Families take care of each other,
- We all have families, and
- Families are all different.

Book reference: *Down the Road* by Alice Schertle, Illustrated by E.B. Lewis
What we are learning…

Understanding Emotions

We read *Down the Road* together and saw how the characters felt at different times during the story. We have been talking about feelings, naming them, and sharing about what makes us feel one way or another. When we did this we learned:

- To describe some of our own feelings,
- To notice that people behave differently at different ages,
- To observe the feelings and behavior of our siblings, our peers, and of adults, and
- To recognize and explore similarities and differences among individuals' and groups' beliefs and feelings.

This Classroom Is for Everyone!

In *This Is Our House*, George made very unfair rules. The other

children worked to create a rule that was fair to all. We discussed

some of our classroom rules and have voted on which rules we think are fair

or not fair. We made a list of classroom rules we all agree to follow.

This Is Our Classroom Museum

After we read *This Is Our House*, we decided to work together to build a classroom

museum. We collaborated on planning, designing, and building our museum. We

learned about:

- Cooperation,
- Needs and wants, and
- Making choices.

Book reference: *Chester's Way* by Kevin Henkes
What we are learning…

Making Friends and Keeping Them

In *Chester's Way*, Chester and Wilson are friends who do everything together. Then Lily moves into the neighborhood. Chester and Wilson learn that even though Lily does things differently, she is a true friend.

In this exploration we learned:

- Friends are special people,
- Friends help each other, and
- Friends do fun things together.

FOR FAMILIES
Book reference: *Chester's Way* by Kevin Henkes
What we are learning…

I Like This, You Like That

After reading *Chester's Way* we made some graphs and discovered that, just like Chester, Wilson, and Lily, we each have our own likes and dislikes. We are unique individuals but we also share many of the same traits and interests.

We talked about how:

- We all like to do things our way,
- We can learn to like new things and new ways,
- Friends can like different things and still be friends,
- Friends can like similar things, and
- A graph can show us a lot of information.

FOR FAMILIES
Book reference: *Jamaica and Brianna* by Juanita Hill,
Illustrated by Anne Sibley O'Brien
What we are learning:

I Like You Because...

We have been reading *Jamaica and Brianna,* a book about friends. We are continuing our exploration of friendship by writing poems. Each of us wrote a poem called, "I Like You Because…." about a friend. The poems were bound into a class book. Please ask to borrow this book so your family can enjoy reading it together. By thinking about friendship and writing poems about it we are learning:

- What characteristics we think are special,
- How we are the same and different, and
- To remember the past and imagine the future.

FOR FAMILIES
Book reference: *Jamaica and Brianna* by Juanita Hill,
Illustrated by Anne Sibley O'Brien
What we are learning:

It's a Shoe-in!

After reading *Jamaica and Brianna* we became shoe designers. We talked about what we needed for our shoe designs, and then we created our shoes. When we were done we made a shoe store in the room and pretended to buy and sell our special shoes. We talked about:

- What special things we need for our shoes,
- How different kinds of shoes have special features,
- What a shoe store is like, and
- How to buy and sell things.

FOR FAMILIES

Book reference: *Officer Buckle and Gloria* by Peggy Rathmann

What we are learning…

How Do You Do, Officer?

We read *Officer Buckle and Gloria* and we wanted to learn more about a real-life police officer, so we invited Officer _____ to visit our class. The police officer told us how she makes sure people in our community are safe. Here are some things we learned about:

- How people must follow the rules to stay safe,
- What police officers wear and the special equipment they carry, and
- What officers do in their jobs.

FOR FAMILIES

Book reference: *Officer Buckle and Gloria* by Peggy Rathmann

What we are learning…

Safety Rules

After reading *Officer Buckle and Gloria*, we talked about what we would like on a playground and what rules we would have so everyone could have a good time and be safe. We learned about:

- Becoming effective problem solvers and decision makers,
- Rules for keeping us safe, and
- Being responsible.

Book reference: *Guess Who?* by Margaret Miller

What we are learning…

Mural of Community Helpers

We've been reading *Guess Who?* and studying workers in our community. We painted a mural of the neighborhood and then put workers in it. We learned that:

- Our community is where we live,
- Workers help their community by doing important jobs,
- Some workers' jobs are to keep us safe or take care of us, and other workers' jobs provide us with things we need, and
- People earn money doing their jobs, and use it to pay for the things their families need.

Book reference: *Guess Who?* by Margaret Miller

What we are learning…

Let's Be Researchers!

After we read *Guess Who?* we took a field trip to find out about _____.

_____ helped make this a very smooth and interesting learning experience.

- We wanted to know what the business _____, who does the work, why they do it and how they do it. As researchers, we
- Explored some jobs done by workers in our community,
- Asked questions, and
- Learned that people use tools and machines to make their jobs easier.

We Produce and We Buy

We had so much fun reading *Bunny Money* that we decided to make our own store.
First, we had to make _____ in our factory, and then we set up a
shop. Customers came and bought our product.
We learned that:

- People work in factories,
- Factories produce things for stores to sell,
- People work in stores, and
- Stores sell things to people who want or need them.

FOR FAMILIES

Book reference: *Bunny Money,* by Rosemary Wells
What we are learning…

The Further Adventures of Max and Ruby

After we read *Bunny Money* we decided to write another adventure starring Max
and Ruby. We learned that most stories have a problem to be solved. Max and Ruby
have a BIG problem in our story! As we followed our favorite bunny characters, we
also learned about:

- The difference between needs and wants,
- Saving and spending money, and
- Making choices about money.

FOR FAMILIES
Book reference: *I Stink!* by Kate and Jim McMullan
What we are learning…

Collecting Garbage

Reading *I Stink!* got us thinking about garbage. Where does all the garbage go? We talked about our classroom garbage and made a chart showing what we could recycle or reuse.

As we sorted and talked, we thought about:

- Our impact on the environment,
- How our actions can help keep our world clean, and
- Ways to reuse materials to cut down on waste.

FOR FAMILIES
Book reference: *I Stink!* by Kate and Jim McMullan
What we are learning…

Build a Vehicle

Reading *I Stink!* made us curious about different kinds of vehicles and what people use them for. We built vehicles in the classroom. As we did this we talked about:

- How we have vehicles for different purposes, and
- The kinds of specialized tools and vehicles workers use to do their jobs.

For Families

Book reference: *The Little Red Hen (Makes a Pizza)* by Philemon Sturges,
Illustrated by Amy Walrod
What we are learning…

Role Play

We read *The Little Red Hen (Makes a Pizza)* and then we acted out the story. In the story, nobody cooperates with the Little Red Hen in making the pizza, but they are all ready to help eat it!

Here are some social studies ideas we are learning about:

- Understanding the difference between things we want and things we need,
- Making decisions based on money and resources,
- Understanding the balance between rights and responsibilities, and
- Understanding how an individual can make a positive difference in the community.

For Families

Book reference: *The Little Red Hen (Makes a Pizza)* by Philemon Sturges,
Illustrated by Amy Walrod
What we are learning…

Create a Restaurant

After reading *The Little Red Hen (Makes a Pizza)* we began thinking about restaurants and the people who work in them. We decided to set up a restaurant in our classroom. We talked about:

- The different jobs people who work in restaurants do,
- How all of the restaurant workers cooperate in order to be successful,
- How a restaurant needs customers so it can earn money to pay the workers, and
- How customers pay money for the food they eat and the service they receive.

Map Your Classroom

After reading *My Map Book,* we made a map of our classroom. We worked hard to include the important things about our room. When we were done, we used the map to help people get from place to place.

When we made and used this map we practiced:

- Matching objects to geographical locations,
- Using location words such as *between, around, next to,* and
- Using symbols to stand for objects.

Map Your Neighborhood

We've been exploring *My Map Book* and learning how to make maps. In order to know the neighborhood, we went on a walk and made a map of our route. We learned that maps are special pictures that represent a place. When we made maps, we practiced:

- Using our personal experiences to explore concepts about places,
- Using locational words such as *around, next to, behind,* and
- Following a map to get from one place to another.

Book reference: *To Be a Kid* by Maya Ajmera and John D. Ivanko

What we are learning…

A Kid Is a Kid Is a Kid

We have been using *To Be a Kid* to see how children all over the world are alike and different. We've been looking at how children in other countries play, spend time with their families, and go to school. We found the countries on the map and globe. We have:

- Compared characteristics and behaviors of people in different counties,
- Learned that there are different nations with different traditions and practices, and
- Explored what activities are common to people around the world.

Book reference: *To Be a Kid* by Maya Ajmera and John D. Ivanko

What we are learning…

Globe Toss!

We read *To Be a Kid* and looked at a globe to find some of the places the children in the book live. We played a game called "Globe Toss!" and we practiced recognizing land and water on the globe.

We also learned that:

- A globe is a kind of a map,
- A globe is like a picture of the whole world,
- Different places on the globe are labeled with words,
- Water (oceans and seas) is blue on the globe, and
- Land is other colors on the globe.

Getting to School

We read *Where Are You Going Manyoni?* and discovered that Manyoni walks a long distance, passing wild animals, on her way to school every day. It made us think about the different ways we get to school. We made a graph of our findings and we update it every morning. By doing this exploration, we learned that there are many ways to get to school.

FOR FAMILIES

Book reference: *Where Are You Going Manyoni?* by Catherine Stock

What we are learning…

Same and Different Routines

We read *Where Are You Going Manyoni?* and learned that everyone has routines.

We made a book about our daily routines. By doing this exploration, we learned:

- People have their own routines,
- Some of our routines are the same as others' routines, and
- Some of our routines are different from others' routines.

INDEX OF CHILDREN'S BOOKS

INDEX

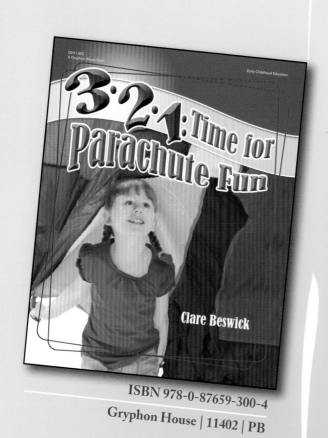

ISBN 978-0-87659-300-4

Gryphon House | 11402 | PB

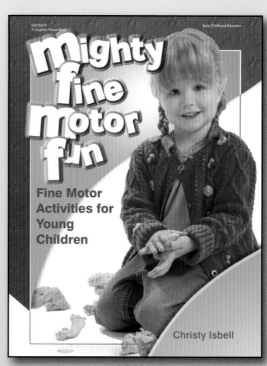

ISBN 978-0-87659-079-9

Gryphon House | 13679 | PB

ISBN 978-0-87659-006-5

Gryphon House | 11308 | PB

ISBN 978-0-87659-317-2

Gryphon House | 10722 | PB

ISBN 978-0-87659-358-5

Gryphon House | 13530 | PB

ISBN 978-0-87659-053-9

Gryphon House | 18492 | PB

ISBN 978-0-87659-064-5

Gryphon House | 13365 | PB

ISBN 978-0-87659-068-3

Gryphon House | 18345 | PB

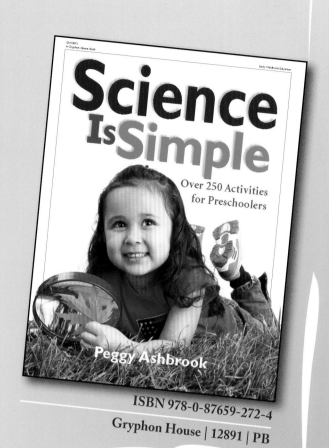

ISBN 978-0-87659-272-4

Gryphon House | 12891 | PB

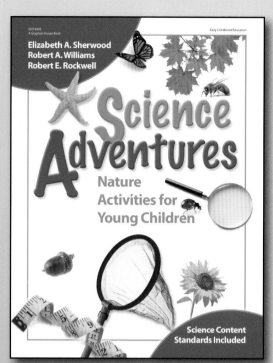

ISBN 978-0-87659-015-7

Gryphon House | 19436 | PB

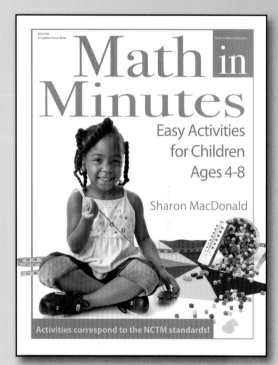

ISBN 978-0-87659-057-7

Gryphon House | 12795 | PB

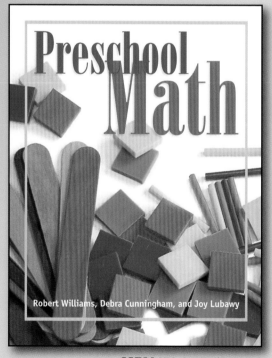

ISBN 978-0-87659-000-3

Gryphon House | 12753 | PB

I Love Letters!

More Than 200
Quick & Easy Activities
to Introduce Young Children
to Letters and Literacy

Jean Feldman and
Holly Karapetkova

ISBN 978-0-87659-080-5

Gryphon House | 19206 | PB

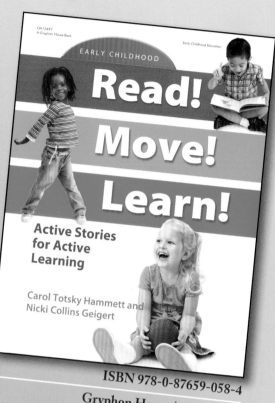

EARLY CHILDHOOD

Read! Move! Learn!

Active Stories
for Active
Learning

Carol Totsky Hammett and
Nicki Collins Geigert

ISBN 978-0-87659-058-4

Gryphon House | 13497 | PB

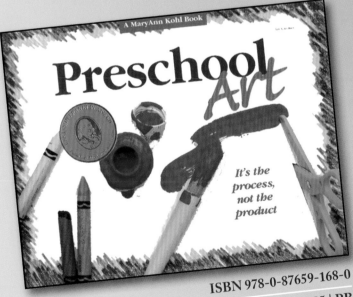

A MaryAnn Kohl Book

Preschool Art

It's the
process,
not the
product

ISBN 978-0-87659-168-0

Gryphon House | 16985 | PB

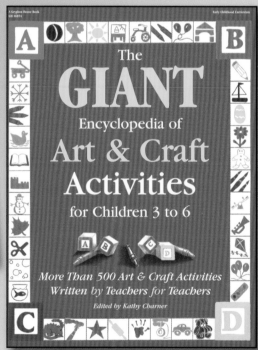

The
GIANT
Encyclopedia of
Art & Craft
Activities
for Children 3 to 6

More Than 500 Art & Craft Activities
Written by Teachers for Teachers

Edited by Kathy Charner

ISBN 978-0-87659-209-0

Gryphon House | 16854 | PB